Joyful Nordic Humor

En brudeford, 1887

This illustration, by Theodore Kittelsen, is a parody on a famous Norwegian painting of a "Bridal Party" on the Hardanger Fjord.

Courtesy of Vesterheim,
Norwegian-American Museum, Decorah, Iowa

Dragon Head
Carved by Elmer Adolf Olsen.
In the collection of Vesterheim, Norwegian-American Museum,
Decorah, Iowa.

Joyful Nordic Humor
a family album

Nordic Heritage
Celebrations, Humor, Jokes, Folk Art, Photographs

Compiled by Joan Liffring-Zug Bourret

Includes entries by

Robin Ouren

Garrison Keillor

Anders Neumueller

and

*David Belgum, Joan Liffring-Zug Bourret, Susan Griffith,
Tony Jellich, Inkeri Väänänen-Jensen, Rev. Jonna Jensen,
Bengt G. Johnson, Donna Lee, Dana Lumby,
Gail Carson Mackay, Richard L. Mattson, and John Zug*

Cartoons by David Fitzsimmons

Penfield
Press

*This treasury of humorous recollections, confessions, and antics
is dedicated to Nordic Americans and all
who laugh joyfully with them.*

Special thanks to Darrell Henning, director, and Carol Hasvold, librarian of Vesterheim, Norwegian-American Museum, Decorah, Iowa, for their help with this book. Thank you to Carol Harker, Director of Communications for the University of Iowa Alumni Association; Holly Carver, University of Iowa Press, and Anders Neumueller, Swedish Press, for permissions to reprint from their publications. Thanks to Theresa Aho, John and Gerry Kangas, and Brenda Van Bergen, Jean and Jim Smith for their special help. We also thank the writers of essays and those who shared memories, expertise, news of events and notable occasions as noted throughout the book.

Compiled by Joan Liffring-Zug Bourret, Penfield Press publisher. Joan began her career as a photographer at the age of fifteen, subsequently combining education and professional endeavors in journalism, public relations and publishing. Her work as a photographer has been recognized as a significant contribution to documenting the history and culture of an era, meriting a place in the Iowa Women's Hall of Fame.

Writer Robin Ouren lives in the tiny northeast Iowa hamlet of Waterville, with very Norwegian-American husband Eric and daughter Beret. She is a graduate of Bethany Lutheran College, Mankato, Minnesota, and Luther College, Decorah, Iowa, with a degree in Theatre Arts, which she says comes in handy while playing the roles of full-time mom and wife, part-time writer, part-time defender of justice, and once in a great while, birdwatcher.

Writer Dana Lumby has a degree in Fine Arts from Iowa State University, Ames, Iowa. With both Swedish and Norwegian ancestry, Dana is the product of a tradition of mixed marriages.

Associate editors: Greta Anderson, Melinda Bradnan, Miriam Canter, Jean Caris-Osland, Dorothy Crum, Esther Feske, Georgia Heald, Eric Heskje, Dana Lumby and Harry Oster.
Graphic design editors: Greta Anderson, Dana Lumby, Walter Meyer.

Front cover photograph, by Melvin M. Scott, Jr., taken at *Norsk Høstfest*, Minot, North Dakota, shows Charlene Power, the Queen Lena of the *Ole and Lena* joke books, Crosby, North Dakota, with Jean and Milton Odden of "Odden's Norsk Husflid," Barronette, Wisconsin, wearing troll costumes from Norway. Back cover photograph by John Zug. Photographs throughout by Joan Liffring-Zug Bourret, John Johnson, and others as noted. Cartoons by David Fitzsimmons, Tucson, Arizona.

© Penfield Press 1997 — Library of Congress 97-65662 — ISBN 1-57261-051-9

Introduction
Joyful Nordic Roots

Of the many ethnic groups in America, the Scandinavians and Finnish people seem to have the most public fun. An inherent security and confidence that allows them to laugh at themselves possibly comes from being descended from the Vikings, once the terror of coastlines from northern Europe to Sicily. They have a long, unique tradition as American immigrants who have dared to make fun. They do not hold themselves sacred. They have a secure sense of who they are.

Nordic people tend to be stoic and serious in their native countries. Nordic fun is an American "New World" phenomenon. Who but the Norwegians would have Ole and Lena jokes? Some say Lena should have divorced Ole years ago, but when they divided up their worldly goods, who would have gotten the best jokes? That might not be a joking matter.

The Nordic people's love of fancy and fantasy has radiated worldwide in the tradition of trolls and nisser. The first artist to picture humorous trolls and funny illustrations of creatures was Theodore Kittelsen, turn of the century Norwegian artist. Walt Disney visited Tivoli, the great Copenhagen, Denmark amusement park before creating Disneyland in Southern California. His mentor was Alfred Tengren, a Swedish artist who was on speaking terms with the dwarfs and Snow White even though they were of German folklore origin. Tengren worked for a time for Disney.

Touches of the Old Country

Yearnings to exist with touches of heritage are seen in many ways. Eric Bye, of an Oslo, Norway radio station, composed a song about the Norwegian immigrant in the Dakota plains who missed the mountains so much that he built a big hill in his yard. According to Darrell Henning, Director of Vesterheim, the Norwegian-American Museum in Decorah, Iowa, concrete *kubbestoler* (a design for a one-piece chair traditionally made from a single log) are on a farmstead in Minnesota.

5

A Proud Heritage

Seattle's Nordic Heritage Museum features all the northern European people from Denmark, Finland, Iceland, Norway, Sweden, and also the Sami who roam freely the lands around the Arctic Circle. The city of Seattle, in recognition of Nordic heritage and in keeping with Native American heritage, presented the gift of a totem pole to its sister city, Bergen, Norway.

The Finnish people kept their identity in spite of over 500 years of Swedish domination, then Russian control. They preserved their own language, non-Germanic, which differentiates them from Scandinavians and the adjacent Slavic peoples. Linked by land to Sweden, they looked west for political freedom. "Finns have always been a contradiction," according to Professor Emeritus Marion Nelson of the University of Minnesota and former director of Vesterheim.

A testament to Finnish-American spirit is St. Urho. St. Urho? a Finnish saint conceived at a department store in Virginia, Minnesota, whose day is celebrated to rival St. Patrick. There are those who say the creators of St. Urho did not like the green of the rival saint. Others point out that not one grasshopper has been seen in Finland since the creation of St. Urho. Of course, no grasshoppers were seen in Finland before St. Urho who stalked the lands after the last ice age. This is cited to show the great — national — international — need for a St. Urho.

The photographs in this album, taken at festivals and events, portray fun-loving Nordic Americans. Artifacts pictured are in private or museum collections. Look and read on, and you'll learn more than you ever thought you wanted to know about Scandinavian and Finnish fun and how catching — how contagious it can be.

> — *Joan Liffring-Zug Bourret, publisher Penfield Press,*
> *great granddaughter of Gunhild Gunderson,*
> *Norwegian immigrant, 1865**

Warning: **Marilyn Skaugstad, of Iowa City, Iowa, Norwegian-American, says any Norwegian ancestry tends to be dominant for any number of generations!*

Entries

Is the problem lutefisk?

"The Tabby Cat Who Ate Such a Terrible Lot"

Drawing by Theodore Kittelsen, late 19th-century Norwegian artist, and one of the first Nordic artists to introduce humor into his work.

Courtesy of Vesterheim, Norwegian-American Museum, Decorah, Iowa

Joke along with
Our Joyful Nordic Cover Girl

Queen Lena, Immigrant Wife

By John Zug

They call her Queen Lena, and she is noted for her Norwegian jokes. Charlene Power of Crosby, North Dakota, finds that a joke on the Norwegians is appreciated most by the Norwegians themselves. "They have a sense of humor and like to tell jokes on themselves," she says.

Charlene, a grandmother, says she would like more than anything to have a Norwegian ancestry, but it is too late now. She is of English and Irish descent. "At least, my mother-in-law is 100 percent Norwegian!" Her husband is half-Norwegian.

Charlene has hosted the "Crosby Hour" on Tioga's Radio Station KTGO for fourteen years. It was on this show that she came to be identified with Norwegian jokes. "People phoned in the jokes," she said, "and we used them."

Charlene's jokes can be told with confidence to your grandmother or your child. Her first book was titled *Uff-da*. It was followed in 1977 by *The New Uffda*, in 1981 by *Ya Sure, You Betcha*, in 1984 by *Leapin' Lena*, in 1990 by *Love, Lutefisk, and Lena*, and in 1994 by *The Best of Queen Lena*. In 1996 she released *Lena Loves Ole Jokes Uff-da #7, A Collection of 247 3/4 Scandinavian Jokes.*

"I don't want to overdo it," she says. "I probably have already." Among those who like her books are ministers, some of whom refer to her jokes in sermons.

Full of Fun

One of her stories tells of a man who plowed up a mirror, looked at it, and said, "Hmmm, I never knew my fadder had his picture taken!" He hung it in the attic, and often went up to take another look. This made his wife curious. When he was out in the field, she went up, looked at the mirror, and said to herself, "Vell. So dat's da old hagg he's been running around vit!"

A Norwegian told the immigration officer his name was Ole Olson. Asked his name, the next Norwegian said, "sam ting." His name has been Sam Ting ever since.

Hilda took the biggest piece of cake. Lena said, "That vasn't very polite of you."
"Vell, vat vould you have done?"
"I vould have been polite and taken the smaller vun."
"Vell, that is vat you have, so why complain?"

Little Lena to minister: "Vell, I am glad you came. Now Papa can dew da trick he said he vould do."
Minister: "What's that?"
Little Lena: "Papa said if you came he vould climb da vall!"

Little Lena: "Grandpa, are yew still growing?"
Grandpa: "Why do you ask, Lena?"
Little Lena: "Because da top of your head is coming tru your hair!"

Signs of the Times

Restaurant billboard outside Grand Marais, Minnesota, a jump from the Canadian border, features Italian and Mexican food instead of lutefisk and lefse. A sign of the cross-cultural Americanization of Scandinavians Sven and Ole, Inga and Lena.

Searching for Nordic Americans

By Robin Ouren

How do you recognize people who are Nordic? Here are some of the telltale signs that will give you a clue:

1. They have last names such as Andersen, Anderson, Larsen, Larson, Petersen, Peterson, Jensen, Johnson, Jarvenpa, Aho, Hillila....
2. They buy insurance from places with names like Lutheran Brotherhood, Danish Brotherhood, Norwegian Mutual....
3. They can be found at church basement dinners — oftentimes first in line.
4. They may be eating an open-face sandwich.
5. The women spend hours upon hours in the kitchen around Christmas, baking *riisipuuro* (Finnish rice pudding), *kringle* (Danish pastry consisting of thirty-some layers of dough, filled with fruit, butterscotch, raisins, or nuts), or *sandbakkels* (Norwegian cookies, generally filled with berries and whipped cream). Sugar canisters are usually empty when the baking is done.
6. Fruit soup is a favorite treat.
7. All activities are dropped at three o'clock each afternoon to partake in a hearty meal, quite possibly consisting of open-face sandwiches, cake, and lots of coffee. Not to worry if "lunch" did not satisfy your hunger, for supper follows closely behind, as does a bedtime snack.
8. Table runners are used year-round; woven hangings are on the walls.
9. "Leif landed first!" is proudly proclaimed with full knowledge that Leif Ericson, Viking explorer, landed in North America in 1002, nearly 500 years before Columbus.
10. They will know that Snorri Sturluson, thirteenth-century Icelandic historian and poet, wrote *Prose Edda*, the definitive work on Norse mythology. Most of what we know about Norse myths, gods, and legends is derived from this work.

Norse Gods

Drawings by Norma Wangsness from *Nils Discovers America* by Julie Jensen McDonald.

Odin the Supreme Deity, creator of world and man. God of wisdom, war, art, culture, and the dead, he lives in Valhalla, Norse heaven for heroic warriors.

Loki, Norse mischief maker, creator of discord among the gods

Frey, Norse god of peace, good weather, prosperity, and bountiful crops

Thor, god of thunder

11. They will recognize or be familiar with *The Kalevala*, the national Finnish epic poem based on oral poetry, collected and first published by Elias Lönnrot.
12. If quizzed, they will know the following figures important in Scandinavian history:

Harald Bluetooth (Gormsson): Ruled in Denmark from 935-985 A.D. He united the countries of Denmark and Norway.

Frey: Norse god of peace, good weather, prosperity, bountiful crops.

Odin: Supreme Deity. Creator of the world and man, god of wisdom, war, art, culture, and the dead.

Gorm the Old: Father of Harald Bluetooth. King of Denmark from whom all of the rulers of that country have descended.

Iduna or Idun: Mythological goddess who guarded the golden apples of the gods. The apples gave the gods their eternal youth.

Thor: God of Thunder. Thursday is named for Thor.

Loki: Chief mischief-maker among the gods.

Gustavus Vasa: Ruled in Finland 1523-1560. Led the Reformation in that country, which resulted in the organization of the Finnish-Lutheran Church.

Eric the Red: Viking explorer. Discovered Greenland, 982 AD.

St. Mårten: Swedish Americans start the holiday season on November 10, the traditional St. Mårten's Gos Day, symbolizing prosperity and good cheer, with a flourish in Chicago's Andersonville Swedish area.

Santa Lucia: Lucia of Sicily. She was among the early 4th-century Christian martyrs. Legend says that several hundred years later, she appeared and brought food to famine-ravaged Sweden.

St. Urho: Mythological Finnish-American saint. Finnish Americans emerge with the colors of green and purple, and behold grasshoppers on St. Urho's Day, March 16.

Roots Revisited

Tracing one's ancestry is a popular pursuit. Americans care about who they really are and where they came from. Filling in the family tree, looking up your genealogy, can be an exciting and interesting endeavor, especially for Scandinavians.

My great grandfather and his brothers emigrated from Sweden to the United States. Some came by way of New York, others Canada. Five brothers, all named Johnson, no, wait!—in the old country, it was Johannson, or Jenson or something like that—somehow it was mistakenly written as Johnson, so some of the records going back have one name, and some the other. Of course, when my great grandfather and his brothers got here and discovered that everyone else in the country was also named Johnson, and no one was getting the right mail because of it, they all decided to change their last names. They each took different names, and scattered out around the Midwest. My great grandfather chose his name by adding a "T" to the front of someone else's name and became Frank Tolander.

This is not an attempt to confuse later generations of ancestor detectives. I just wanted to learn about who they were, not play "Mission Impossible."

Luckily, someone else in my family had written pages of names on lines attached to other lines, with arrows connecting people, and dates written down, then scribbled out and rewritten somewhere else. This is standard for a "Family Tree."

Then there were the Norwegians. The other side of my family history was just as confusing. Scandinavians, especially Norwegians, used patrilineal names. The explanation is that they were trying to ensure that their names lived on, but I know better. Let's see, Olav Olavson was Olav, the son of Olav. Katrina Torbjørnsdatter was Katrina, the daughter of Torbjørn. Okay, that's easy. Olav's first son was named Hans. Hans was called Hans Olavson. Hans had a son. He named him Olav Hanson, or Olav, son of Hans. Hans had a son, and his name was? Yes, Olav Hanson! This could go on for decades. And did. Until they came to America.

They found that the mail system in the New World messed up things for the Norwegians too, so everyone took different names, sometimes names from the area where they lived in the old country—names that you can hardly pronounce, like Åkre, Djønne, or Hjørnevig. Someone in my family decided to put up with getting the wrong mail and stayed with Larson—which, of course, is not the correct Norwegian spelling. Norwegian names end with "sen," and Swedish names end in "son." But, the mail problem prompted changes like these too.

All of this certainly makes researching one's ancestry difficult. Imagine inquiring about Hans Olavson. Which one? Hans, the father of Olav Hanson, or Hans, the son of Olav Hanson? And don't forget, sometimes two siblings shared the same name, sort of like Dr. Seuss's "Thing One" and "Thing Two." Or, one son died in infancy, an unfortunately common occurrence until fairly recently, and the next son was given the same name.

Another interesting and confusing element I stumbled across in digging for roots is the notorious double cousin syndrome. Defined: a double cousin is a person who is your first cousin on both your mother's side and your father's side of the family. Explained further, your dad's sister or brother married one of your mom's sisters or brothers. So, two siblings are married to two siblings. These couples have children. The children are double first cousins, related on both sides of the family. My great grandfather Edward, his sister Elise, and brother Holger, married, respectively: Mathilda, Johan, and Caroline Anderson. These three couples had many children, and for an entire generation of the family, everyone was related twice. Being kin to some relatives once is enough.

I managed to figure out all of "my first cousins once removed" (my parents' first cousins), but as for my "shirt-tail relations," as Grandma Tolander calls them, that was a branch I did not attempt to explore. Familiarizing myself with just the trunk and major limbs on my gnarled and knotted family tree was too much like trying to learn all of the declensions in Latin.

15

Anyway, by the time the genealogy fad comes around again in this country, people will be digging way back to the 1960s and writing things on their family trees like: "Moonbeam (no last name), daughter of Free Spirit and (father unknown). Maybe dealing with the Olav Olavsons isn't so bad after all.

Anyone seriously interested in finding their Nordic roots can begin or continue their search at such places as:

Danes: The Danish Immigrant Museum
Family History and Genealogical Center
P.O. Box 470
Elk Horn, Iowa 51531

Norwegians: Vesterheim Genealogical Center
Naeseth Library
415 West Main Street
Madison, Wisconsin 53703-3116

Swedes: Swenson Swedish Immigration
Research Center - Augustana College
Denkman Memorial Library
Rock Island, Illinois 61201

Finns: Finnish American Heritage Center
Suomi College
601 Quincy Street
Hancock, Michigan 49930

Also helpful: Family History Library
35 North West Temple Street
Salt Lake City, Utah 84150

Happy hunting and fishing!

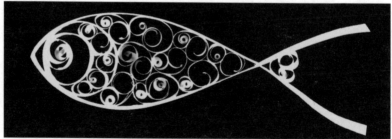

Lastucraft fish made of pine shavings by the Ladies of Kaleva, Virginia, Minnesota

From Fantastically Finnish:
Recipes and Traditions

Visiting the Old Countries
Wish you were here!

Troll in the Mountain, Stalheim, Norway. Norwegians historically found trolls lurking in nature. Today, they lock doors and cupboards as protection against trolls?

Troll at the train station, Flam, Norway, waiting to emigrate to America. In the meantime, the troll pleasantly poses with Teddy Ellison, American tourist from California.

Turku, Finland

Runeberg Park

Michael G. Karni, Ph.D., editor of *Finnish Americana*, stands next
to "Lilja," created in 1928 by sculptor Wäinö Aaltonen. "Lilja" is
in perpetual anticipation, waiting in Runeberg Park in the city of
Turku, Finland, for Paavo Nurmi, the great Olympic champion,
to run to her side. Students drape her with their graduation caps
on Vappu Day (the first of May) each year.

Photograph ©1994, Seppo Sarimo from *The Best of Finnish Ame*

Discover the American West
Visit Legoland in Denmark!

buffalo cow and calf

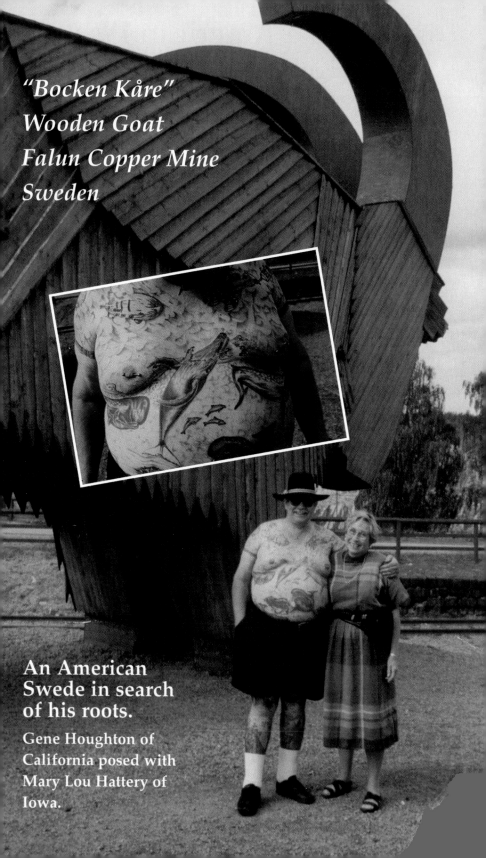

"Bocken Kåre"
Wooden Goat
Falun Copper Mine
Sweden

**An American
Swede in search
of his roots.**

Gene Houghton of
California posed with
Mary Lou Hattery of
Iowa.

American Tourists

By Joan Liffring-Zug Bourret

While on a tour of Norway, Sweden, and Denmark with Anderson Scandinavian Tours of Lindsborg, Kansas, fellow tourist, Mary Lou Hattery of Cedar Rapids, Iowa, and I were enjoying the wonders of the countryside in Norway and relishing a wonderful smorgasbord feast, when we met a remarkable man sitting beside a fjord.

"I'm tattooed from my neck to my ankles," said Gene Houghton of Sacramento, California, explaining that he considers the "tattoo" an art form and that the designs were done by a tattoo artist in California. He explained that his arms, from the elbows down have no tattoos, so in most normal street clothes the art is covered—but he did see a photograph of his knees displayed in a tattoo salon in London!

This was not a surprise to Gene. He has garnered international acclaim through a number of recognitions and awards including: Enthusiast of the Year at the 1986 National Tattoo Association show; Best Overall Tattooed Male, 1994 Living Art Association; features in *National Tattoo Association News* and *Skin and Ink* magazine; also noted in a Time-Life book. Gene says he has stopped entering contests, noting: "After you have won a big award, why enter?"

An obvious attraction on the tour, Gene almost caused car wrecks at a rest stop in Sweden, as the drivers gawked at this man in shorts with whales on his tummy. He noted that in Hawaii the natives were wild about his tattoos; they especially liked the whales since they are the state animal. "With ten whales on the front of me, there was great interest!" he said.

The male goat, Bocken Kåre (opposite page), was installed when the Falun Copper Mine celebrated its 700th Anniversary in 1988. Legend claims that a goat scraped the ground with his horns which turned red, thus the discovery of copper in Sweden. Today, souvenir replica goats sold in Falun have red horns, according to Mana Feldt of the Swedish Information Service, Consulate General of Sweden.

21

"Would you pose for a photo?" I asked. And pose he did with Mary Lou by a wooden goat at a copper mine in Sweden.

Both Gene and his wife Bev are of Swedish descent. Gene's great-grandmother, Anna Marie Nilsson, came from Halmsted, Sweden, where her father was the lighthouse keeper. In finding roots today, Gene said that locating his Nilssons is like trying to find a Jones in Wales. Emphasizing their Swedish roots, they shared a bread recipe brought from Sweden to America by Bev's grandmother, over 100 years ago. Converted by the Houghtons for use in a bread baking machine, the recipe is:

Swedish Raisin Rye Bread

1 package dry yeast
2 cups Better for Bread flour
1 cup rye flour
1/8 cup brown sugar, packed
2 Tablespoons molasses
1 teaspoon anise seed

2 Tablespoons grated
   orange rind
1 teaspoon salt
1 1/2 Tablespoons butter
1 cup very warm water
1 cup raisins

Place all ingredients, except raisins, into the inner pan of breadmaker in the order listed. Select White Bread and push Start. Add raisins when the machine beeps.

Hints:
—1/2 cup regular and 1/2 golden raisins add variety.
—Heat the molasses with water in the microwave to 105 degrees before using. This helps the molasses flow better.
—A suggestion for successfully using the bread machine is to have it go on the short cycle and in the manual mode. When the cycle is finished, turn the dough out onto a floured cookie sheet. Press it into a flat circle, about 10 inches across and 3/4 inch or so thick. Turn on the oven at 200 degrees for two minutes and then off. Place the dough that has been covered with a dish towel in the oven for an hour. After the bread has risen for the hour, bake in a 350 degree oven for 30 minutes.

Gene says, "This bread smells and tastes just like bread I remember some fifty years ago from the Swedish Bakery in South Berkeley, California, and it is WONDERFUL!"

News from Scandinavia

Racial Tension: Milk and a Cow!
An Official "Tail"

Edited by Dana Lumby

This is an abbreviation of a true story that appeared in a number of newspapers. Some regarded it as serious "racial tension," but to the Swedes and Norwegians, it's a family "feud!"

Recently, in a Norwegian courtroom, a court case was being settled over how to milk a cow.

We all know a good Ole and Lena joke, and how to learn to laugh at ourselves, but this case was not just a joke for the parties involved. It all started with a gallon of ice cream.

Norwegians love ice cream. So do the Swedes. So much so that two ice cream makers, one from Norway, one from Sweden, were battling, not with ice cream scoopers, but with television advertisements. A Norwegian company made a television commercial that had the cow's milk curdling.

In the commercial were Swedish men trying to figure out the secret to the Norwegian ice cream. Their attempts would make any cow run for the pastures. One Swede tries to get milk by pumping the cow's tail, another says, "I'm not sick, I'm just Swedish."

You can imagine how amusing the Swedes found this.

This takes us into the courtroom. The Swedish, upon viewing the commercial, accused the Norwegian ice cream company of inciting racial hatred.

The judge's ruling: The commercial was banned on the technicality that there were no specifics on the contents of the Norwegian ice cream.

Despite the ruling, both sides felt victorious. The Norwegian company claimed, "The decision clearly states that we can continue to fight for Norwegian jobs and Norwegian products."

The Swedish company said, "Now we should get more respect. Our sales people have been bullied and called Swedish rogues."

One columnist added that, in America, such a "hate crime" as accusing someone of not knowing how to milk a cow, might lead to compensation for the hurt feelings of the cows!

This cow float was in a **Syttende Mai** *(May 17 celebration) parade in Stoughton, Wisconsin, where the cow is an important figure in the area's dairy production.*

A Lot of Bull

February 1995, a dad in Sweden broke the records at the age of ten! With 92,000 of his kids absent, you could say his birthday party was a flop! Rather, colleagues from Swedish Breeders *(Svensk Avel)* in Skara visited the lowland bull "238 Rögild."

This Danish bull broke all breeding records: during a five year period, and 240,000 doses of sperm later, the ten-year-old bull is still active. A bull's average lifespan is seven or eight years. Way to go 238 Rögild!

Submarines?

Information from *Nordstjernan,* February 16, 1995
Published by *Swedish News*

For some time after World War II, there were numerous reports of evidence of foreign submarines along Sweden's shores. Only one submarine ever surfaced, which was returned to the Soviet Union, but this led to increased speculation that there were indeed undersea intruders. Swedish government officials wrote a very sharp note to Russian officials, verifying that much evidence proved the continued presence of underwater craft.

Military expertise, time, and money were spent tracking the signs of underwater disturbance. This led to new evidence indicating that schools of swimming minks were very likely the cause of many of the underwater sounds!

Along with the many red faces, there is now the question as to how minks may be classified among the defensive or offensive weapons in Sweden's arsenal.

Scandi-*name*-ians

By Robin Ouren

Scandinavian names are wonderful! Strong, unusual, and terribly underused by Scandinavian parents! Here, for your convenience in choosing a name for your child, is a smattering of unique and under-utilized Scandinavian names, their origins and meanings:

DANISH

Dagmar: "Joy of the Danes." (Pronounced "DOW·mer.")

Dana: "From Denmark."

Gorm: Ancient King of Denmark.

Harald: Son of King Gorm. Brought Christianity to Denmark.

Knute: "Knot." Canute is the Old Norse spelling.

Axel: "Peace loving." Form of Absalom.

FINNISH

Helga: "Pearl."

Lempi: "Love."

Niles: "Victory of the people."

ICELANDIC

Snorri: Name of poet/writer who compiled the mythological epics.

NORTHERN MYTHOLOGY

Balder: Son of Freyja (see reference). He was nearly invincible, impervious to wounds of all kinds except those from mistletoe.

Brynhild: Maiden warrior.

Dofri: A mountain giant who trained Harald Fairhair in ancient lore and aided him in various ways.

Freyja, Frigg: Wife of Odin (see reference). Mother goddess, Queen of heaven. Friday is named for her.

Idun: Goddess who protected the "golden apples" which gave the gods eternal youth.

Loki: Trickster in the world of the gods.

Odin: "Father" of the gods. God of battle and death. Wednesday is named for him.

Sigmund: Dragon-slaying hero in the world of the gods.

Sigurd: Son of Sigmund, another hero.

OLD NORSE

Erik: Erik the Red discovered Greenland in 982. His son, Leif Erikson, discovered North America in 1002. American spelling is Eric.

Be prepared. Children like to participate in "ugly" troll contests. Scene at Syttende Mai, *Stoughton, Wisconsin.*

Garth: "Groundskeeper."
Gunnar: "Warrior." Also Gun, Gunther, Gunner, Gunter. Gustav, Gustave (name of several kings of Sweden). Gustav Vasa brought Christianity to Sweden.
Ingemar: "Famous son."
Inger: "Son's Army."

Olaf: Name of many kings of Norway. Olaf Tryggvason brought Christianity to Norway. Olof is the Swedish spelling. Also Ole, Olav, Olen, Olin.

SWEDISH
Sven: "Youth."
Anna: "Gracious."
Atalie: "Pure."
Kristen: "Anointed."
Ivar: "Archer."

And don't forget to consider Lena, Siri, Kjersti (pronounced CHAIR·stee), Marit, Ingrid, Kari, Signe (pronounced SIG·nee) and Gunhild for girls, and Per, Syvert, Hans, Holger, Nels, Johan, Tosten, and Kristian for boys.

If you still can't settle on the "right" name, take a drive to a Scandinavian-settled community sometime and stop by a little country cemetery. Tombstones are good sources for great old names. I'm sure the occupants won't mind if you borrow their names. They might even be flattered.

27

Our Finnish Names

By Inkeri Väänänen-Jenson, from *My Story, Inkeri's Journey*

In the 1920s we Finns cringed and became
ashamed of our awkward Finnish names.
The girls suffered with Kerttu, Llahja, Lyyli,
Raakeli, Irja, Saima, Helmi, and Taimi.
The Americans had names like
Jean, Jane, Joan, and Nancy.
The boys struggled with Ensio, Poju, Teuvo,
Jorma, Toimi, Toivo, Urho, and Veikko.
The Americans had names like
Jim, Bob, Dick, and Bill.

How could we tell these Americans
That our names were the names of love,
And of our parents' hopes for the future?
Adored One, Songbird, Young Bud, Sonny,
The First One, Hope, Gift, Pearl, Hero,
And even Champion?

Our last names gave us the most trouble.
For we had names from Finland like
Koivumäki, Hirvivaara, Metsäpelto,
Järvenpää, Tuomikoski, Pyylampi.
If birches grew near the house on the hill,
The family name became Koivumäki (Birch Hill).
If elks had once roamed through the high land,
The family took the name of Hirvivaara (Elk Mountain).
If the family field had been wrested from a thick forest,
The name, of course, would be Metsäpelto (Forest Field).
If the house was build at the head of a lake,
The family name became Järvenpää (Lakehead).
If the farm was near a rapids where chokecherries grew,
The name taken would be Tuomikoski (Chokecherry Rapids).
If the farm included a pond where partridges abounded,
The Pyylampi (Partridge Pond) became the family name.

But how could we explain
All this geography, this history.
To our classmates, to our teachers
Who had last names like Brown, Jones, and Smith?

Hva heter du?

(Norse meaning "What's your name?")

By Robin Ouren

My daughter's name is Beret. For the non-Scandinavians out there, that is pronounced BEAR·et. This answers the question of why we named our daughter after the little round caps worn jauntily by Frenchmen in striped shirts. We did not!

"What is your adorable little girl's name?"

"Beret," I say.

"Ferret?"

"No, Beret," I answer, emphasizing the "B" part.

"How unusual, where did that name come from?" people usually ask after they have figured out that Beret's name is not Ferret, Parrot, or Carrot. "The name," I tell them, "is a very, very, very old Norwegian name. The Swedish spelling is B·e·r·i·t." We didn't decide on the spelling until we were in the delivery room cuddling the adorable little person.

"Is there some significance to the name? Was she named for an ancestor?"

"No," I say to people. "Beret is the main character in Ole Edvart Rölvaag's *Giants in the Earth* sagas. Norwegian-born (1876-1931) writer and teacher, Rölvaag immigrated to America and studied at St. Olaf College in Northfield, Minnesota. He taught Norwegian Literature at St. Olaf while writing books about the Norwegian immigrants in America—*Giants in the Earth, Peder Victorious,* and *Their Fathers' God.* Beret and her husband Per Hansa and family homestead with a group of other Norskies out on the very, very flat and very, very windy prairie of the Dakotas, and the sweeping epic saga begins." On the downside, Beret goes insane for a time in the first book. The very flat and very, very windy prairie is a bit much for her. In the other two books, she is, at times, emotionally unstable. But I don't tell people that when they ask about our darling Beret.

Eric and I decided, before the blessed event, that we wanted traditional Scandinavian names and agreed on Beret right away. If it were a boy, we had thought of Peder. Peder is also in the Rölvaag books—Beret's and Per Hansa's youngest boy. He doesn't go crazy, but he does marry an Irish-Catholic girl, which I suppose in those days was about the same thing. But the name Peder, we knew, could cause problems. Both of Eric's sisters have ex-boyfriends named Peter, and we didn't want them to look at our son with vindictive thoughts! After much disagreement, we decided on Elijah. So, what's wrong with a little Hebrew?

We think, now, that when we have another child, if it's a boy, we will name him Grin—then when people ask our children's names, we can say, "Grin and Beret." About the time they're fifteen, they will hate their names worse than zits and chaperoned dates!

Names! There seems to be a trend back to traditional names. My friend Dave Larson (no relation) named his son Leif. My friends Don and Ginny Larson (no relation to Dave or to my family) named their son Thor. Here we have all of these Scandinavians with non-Scandinavian first names giving their children names from Scandinavian history, mythology, or Ole Rölvaag books! Why? Let's ask them:

The phone lines were busy. Let's assume that they all would have given insightful reasons for their choices: "I named my son Leif because as everyone knows Leif Erikson discovered America 500 years before Columbus. In choosing Leif, I hoped to instill in my son a sense of adventure. It is a name, I knew, that he could wear with pride among kids named Johnny, Billy, and Tommy." "Why Thor?" "Well, Thor is the mythological god of thunder, god of the sky, not to mention a famous comic book superhero. I hoped that as he grew up, Thor could think of his name and have visions of grandeur, of super-human powers that would carry him to heights far beyond those possible by mere mortals."

Okay, the real reason? In a country called the "melting pot," where assimilation used to be the goal, a trend now is to be proud of who you are and where you came from. At least, I long for the day when my daughter will sit in a classroom surrounded by kids named Bjorn, Axel, Gunther, Freyja, and Loki!

Bringing Up Nordic Babies

An Interview with Robin Ouren

By Joan Liffring-Zug Bourret

Author Robin Ouren is three quarters Scandinavian—half Norwegian, one quarter Swedish, and another quarter French and English. After assessing her place in this "melting pot"— the United States—she decided it was about time to reassert her Scandinavianness, particularly the Norwegian half. This presented quite a challenge, considering that traditions and customs among Scandinavians and non-Scandinavians have blended over three-hundred-fifty years of immigrants coming to America and mingled through mixed marriages. "Today," says Robin, "there are over seventeen million Americans of Scandinavian descent scratching their heads in absolute confusion as to who they really are, and trying to 'get back to where we once belonged' (to steal a phrase from a famous non-Scandinavian songwriter) as far as ethnicity is concerned."

Importance of Herring

Thankfully, traces of Scandinavianness do shine through on occasion. My own son, David Heusinkveld, who is one-sixteenth Norwegian, (along with Scottish, English, Belgian, German and Dutch) was like a genetic magnet to a bottle of herring sold at a Prairie du Chien, Wisconsin, boat shop. "Have to have it," he said. I was thrilled to see that even one-sixteenth of Norskness could produce this yearning for herring. It was a good sign. However, my one-quarter Swede daughter-in-law hates herring. A thousand years of herring tradition doesn't always come through!

Even those people who proudly profess "ethnic purity" show signs of confusion. Shortly before she died in 1925 at age seventy-five, my 100 percent Norwegian great-grandmother, Gunhilde Gunderson Lang, confessed to my mother, "We are part Irish you know." What does this mean? Did an Irish sailor

31

venture up a fjord and climb a mountain to our family farm, "Korsgarten," to woo and marry a Norsk lass? Or does it mean a venturesome Viking returned with an Irish girl? We shall never know for certain.

Conditioning Baby

Since the birth of her daughter, Beret, Robin and husband Eric have devised a plan for bringing up their Scandinavian babies. "The goal for us," she says, "is to marry off our daughter to a '100 percent Norsky.' In order to achieve this, the process must start at birth, when baby is impressionable."

There are those who consider a Swede married to a Norwegian a mixed marriage. Robin advises parents to "decide which cultural traditions you wish to strive for. If you are mainly Danish and love kringles and butter, then go for that. If Finnish and you love St. Urho, then that is the determining factor. Is Norwegian lefse more important than Swedish meatballs? Do you favor rosemaling over Dala painting? The answers to these questions are helpful in making the tough decision. We have chosen Norwegian, since I am twice as much Norwegian as anything else, and because I married one of those '100 percent Norskies.'"

"Let's say you choose Norwegian, as we did," says Robin. "First, pick a name for baby that is ultra-Norwegian: Beret, Erik, Siri, Sven. Decorate baby's room with Norwegian flags on curtains, crib sheets, walls. The red field with the white and blue cross provides high contrast visual stimulation for newborns, and also serves to indoctrinate the child immediately. This idea holds true for the other Scandinavians too. Danes could use the white and red flag, Finns the blue and white, and Swedes the yellow and blue."

Robin goes on: "Continue, or start, important traditions so baby gets used to them early on. As soon as little Norsk babies can manage rice cereal, mashed lutefisk can be started. Sweets too can help lean a child toward a particular culture and can be used to ply the child. Pastries including *sandbakkels, krumkake* and *rosettes,* and *rømmegrøt* (milk mush, lots of sugar, butter,

32

cinnamon) are all suitable treats for Norwegian toddlers. Of course, sweets abound among the other Scandinavians, too. Sugar content is the key here.

"The plan must spill over into all aspects of the child's life. It is assumed that as a partial Scandinavian you already attend a Lutheran church. If dilution has changed this, it is important to rectify the situation while children are still young. The child will learn to appreciate Scandinavian traditions such as holding hands and walking around the Christmas tree, going to potlucks, summer Bible school, these kinds of things."

"The Norsk plan would also include teaching the child Norwegian as well as English," says Robin. "The hope is that the child will not be able to separate the two languages, and will begin to assume the Norsk identity. This can be helpful later on, as you set books out for them to read—Ibsen plays in the original Norwegian, old Norwegian Synod pastors' sermons, etc.

"Play traditional folk music around the house and encourage the child to learn 'old time dancing.' This will also be helpful later on. As a change of pace, play Grieg. Teens will be particularly receptive to Grieg because of the uniquely Nordic angst inherent in his music. Teens like angst.

"As the teen begins to think of college," says Robin, "lay out brochures from places with names like St. Olaf and Luther College. Remind the child that you are the parent and, as long as you are paying the tuition, you choose where to go. The child may then tell you where to go, but these things happen."

Lutheran Colleges

Of course, a Swedish child would be "encouraged" to attend Gustavus Adolphus College in St. Peter, Minnesota, or Augustana in Rock Island, Illinois. A Danish American child might choose Dana College in Blair, Nebraska. A Finnish-American child might be found at Suomi College in Hancock, Michigan. And don't forget the Concordia College summer language camps for Finnish, Swedish, Norwegian and Danish. These are located in Minnesota, one of the "Scandinavian hubs"

These are located in Minnesota, one of the "Scandinavian hubs" of America. (Other "hubs" include Wisconsin, Iowa, the Dakotas, anywhere considered "the Midwest," and the Pacific Northwest—Oregon and Washington.)

"Once Beret is enrolled in a suitable Scandinavian school," says Robin, "we will encourage her to take part in a cultural exchange program. Getting her to Norway is the surest way to ensure traditional Norwegian values. And since she will already speak the language, eat the food, and know the dances, she will feel right at home there. If this idea fails, there is always the hope that she will meet a clean-cut Norwegian-American on campus.

"If, after all our intensive care, Beret comes home from college one day and introduces us to her fiancé, Guido, we won't despair. There is more than a good chance that Guido is not completely Italian. After all, the Vikings did visit Sicily. We will rest assured that grandparents often have a great influence on grandchildren, and we'll start mashing the lutefisk!"

Beret's dad, Eric Ouren, in a Nisse cut-out. Photograph taken by her mom at Nordic Fest.

34

Uff Da!

By Robin Ouren

Lena: "I went into labor early Wednesday morning, but little Beret wasn't born until almost forty hours later on Thursday night."

Marit: *"Uff da!"*

Uff da. For the benefit of the seriously non-Norwegians, *uff da* is a common Nordic expression which covers a wide range of emotions. Consisting of two syllables, or more precisely two separate sounds, it is the ultimate expression of emotion for the stoic Norwegians who invented it.

Uff da, as used in the dialogue above, means roughly "Oh my, I can't believe you were in labor for nearly two days! You poor dear! The agony of it all! You have my deepest sympathy!" No sense in overreacting or wasting words and time though. A simple raise of an eyebrow and the slight lilt of *"uff da"* declared under the breath suffices.

If the country were ever to elect a Norwegian to the office of Commander in Chief, *"uff da"* would ensure much shorter State of the Union addresses. President Ole Hansen would simply step up to the mike, peruse the latest figures on the budget deficit, shake his head, and mumble *"uff da."* We would all come to understand that simple utterance as a chastisement of the non-Norwegian Lutheran Democrats who spend like maniacs and as a cry to balance the budget by the end of his term. Questions from the press would follow, and we would all get back to our regularly scheduled programming much sooner.

For die-hard Norskies, there are myriad situations to which *"uff da"* is a fitting exclamation point. Hans loses his job and hard times follow for his family. *Uff da.* The car engine freezes up because Johann neglected to add oil. *Uff da.* Erika studied all night for her physics final but did not do well enough to pull an A in the class, or, she pulled a good grade, but the test was a bear and she is exhausted. Either way, *"uff da"* fits.

Less serious situations also elicit *"uff da's."* Indigestion from eating too much lutefisk and lefse at Christmas deserves an *uff da*. So does a sweltering hot Midwest day where you can't remove enough clothing to be comfortable.

But *"uff da"* isn't reserved only for difficult or uncomfortable situations. Many is the time when, noticing an attractive person of the opposite sex strolling by, *"uff da"* has escaped the mouths of enamored young Norskies. In this instance, the universal translation is the ever-popular wolf whistle.

The Uffda Shop

The Uffda Shop in Red Wing, Minnesota, is headquarters for trolls, tomter, nisser, and other favorite Scandinavian items that might evoke an *"uff da!"* The shop, originally started by Dr. and Mrs. Rolf Skyberg, is managed now by their son Arne's wife Sara.

Along with the array of treasures offered at the shop, there are these revelations of a variety of situations that would probably be best addressed with *"uff da!"*

Uff da *carving,* Høstfest, *Minot, North Dakota*

※ Forgetting your mother-in-law's name.

※ Noticing non-Norwegians using lefse for a napkin at a church dinner.

※ Trying to polka to rock 'n roll.

※ Waking yourself with your own snoring in church!

※ Trying to pour two buckets of manure into one bucket.

※ Not visiting the Uffda Shop.

Celebrating Lefse
"Lefse Dagen"

Information from Arne Pederson
President, Starbuck Depot Society

Books have been written, records broken, and days devoted to the praise of lefse. One most notable of these events is *"Lefse Dagen,"* a day in celebration of lefse, held annually in May in Starbuck, Minnesota, located on the western shore of Lake Minnewaska.

Held at the historic site of the Minnesota Northern Pacific Railroad Depot, which has been restored and preserved by the Starbuck Depot Society, *"Lefse Dagen"* commemorates the record-setting world's largest lefsa baked during the 1983 Starbuck Centennial Celebration. Measuring 9 feet 8 inches in diameter and weighing over 70 pounds, this world record lefse is recorded in the Schibsted Book of Records in Norway. The Guiness Book of Records does not have a category for lefse records!

The Depot Society and the Starbuck Study Club sponsor an open house at the depot, caboose, and storehouse museum, offering live entertainment, demonstrations of lefse baking and of the telegraph. Unique festival food favorites include *Värm Pulsa* (Swedish cooks) or *Varme Pølser* (Norwegian cooks), a sausage wrapped in lefse.

Most of the early settlers in this Pope County town of about 1,200 residents were of Swedish or Norwegian descent. Though people of other descents have found the area to their liking, Scandinavian heritage is preserved and celebrated by all through festivals, arts and crafts, and traditions. *Midsommersnattsfest* with music, dancing and a picnic is sponsored by the Sons of Norway annually. *Eple Tiden,* held in September, is a festive event featuring sales of apples and other foods, produce and goods that are natural resources of the area.

The Great Lefse Awakening

By Robin Ouren

Having spent a lifetime believing that some things were constant, the two biggies that come to mind are: God, and lefse. As for God, things remain status quo. And as for lefse, I've had to accept some shocking revelations.

Growing up, I watched Mom and Grandma and other people prepare the potatoes, roll the dough and lay it out on the lefse griddle. I sampled more than a few warm lefse rounds—butter and sugar melting in my mouth and dripping down my face. Nothing like lefse. And I heard and read many times that the end result was completely dependent on having the right potatoes and preparing those *potatoes* just so. POTATOES.

Then I grew up, went off to college, worked and basically squandered my time on nonsense. Eventually, I found myself a nice clean-cut full-blooded American-Norwegian boy, and got married. Life was going to be perfect. I met his family, a nice clean-cut bunch of full-blooded American-Norwegians with names like Ouren and Henderson and Ogdahl. They made fruit soup. They wore Norwegian sweaters. They had maps of Norway on their kitchen walls. They ate lefse!!!

It was Christmas. We were at Eric's Dad's house. They had lefse. It looked different. I smeared on the butter and poured on the sugar. I rolled up the lefse and took a big bite. It was not lefse. It was definitely not lefse. I wondered "What is this stuff, it tastes…not like lefse?" We were newlyweds. I wanted to be polite, so I ate it. Later, I asked Eric, "What was that stuff anyway, it tasted…not like lefse." Eric, 100 percent Norwegian, assured me that it was indeed lefse. Oatmeal lefse! "Could you repeat that?" "Oatmeal lefse," he said too matter-of-factly.

OATMEAL LEFSE??? Norwegians in the Old Country did not grow oatmeal on those stony hillsides; it was potatoes. POTATOES. I scanned my Norwegian recipe books. Not one recipe anywhere in any Norwegian publication for OATMEAL LEFSE. What I *did* find—to my dismay—were recipes for things called Hard Lefse and Hardanger Lefse—recipes that also did not include POTATOES in the list of ingredients. Non-potato lefse? Life was bad. Cynicism set in.

I was in a daze for weeks. Still curious about the origins of oatmeal lefse, I turned to Vesterheim, the Norwegian-American Museum, for assistance. The Textile Curator (they don't have a lefse curator at Vesterheim) suggested their reference library. I looked. No oatmeal lefse! The director and a curator hypothesized that oats, a common crop in Norway, maybe ended up in lefse before potatoes came along and edged them out.

Next I tried Eric's family. His Aunt Dorothy told me that oatmeal lefse came from the Ouren side of the family, back to Eric's Great-Great-Great-Aunt Betsy Lie. I conducted an "Eric's Great Aunt Phonathon" one night and ended up more confused than I started. Great Aunt Bessie from Edina, Minnesota, said they never ate lefse—oatmeal, potato or any other kind during her childhood—her ninety year old sister Berniece from Fargo, North Dakota, agreed. I tried the *other* side of the family, the non-Ourens. Great Aunt Norma said they never ate lefse either. According to her, "Sister Thelma (Eric's grandma, deceased) was the only person in the family who made lefse." As for the history of oatmeal lefse, Norma said, "I think Thelma experimented and put a handful of oatmeal in it."

Oatmeal lefse. Unless I hear otherwise, the idea was a culinary whim that sprang from the mind of Thelma Ouren sometime in the 1930s or 1940s. Maybe there was a potato shortage in St. James, Minnesota, where she and husband Ed (Eric's grandfather, deceased) lived. Who knows? I am told that Thelma's lefse was the hit of ladies aids and circles, and that everyone else who made lefse pounded at her door for the recipe. To the Ouren family, no other kind of lefse existed.

To the Larson family—*my* family, nothing but potato lefse existed. Life was getting worse. I resigned myself to the fact that lefse, of all things, was going to be the one point of contention that Eric and I must endure. Then I thought: "NO!" I knew that Eric had to see the error of his wayward lefse eating history. I could change him. I *had* to change him before we had children and he ruined their discriminating Norwegian tastebuds.

By the time I came to my senses a few years later, our daughter Beret was four months old. I decided that if she shared her mother's good taste, she would come to see oatmeal lefse for what it really is, and I wouldn't have to worry. Then I realized something else: Thelma Ouren is my daughter's Great Grandmother. Thelma Ouren's oatmeal lefse is as much a part of Beret's Norwegian heritage as everything else we will teach her to appreciate. More importantly than all of that, I knew that if I was the person who brought this lefse aberration to the world and it caught on, I could become rich and famous!!

So, without further delay, I bring you the hit of St. James:

Grandma Thelma's Soon-to-be-World-Famous Oatmeal Lefse

Combine the following:
4 cups flour
1/2 cup instant oatmeal
   (old fashioned five minute is too coarse)
3 tsp. salt (or less)
1/2 tsp. sugar (optional)

Mix all together.

In a large pan, combine the following:
2 cups water
2 cups milk
1/2 cup lard
1/4 cup butter
(If you aren't a diehard Norwegian, you may use ALL butter.)

Bring the mix to a boil. Add dry mixture and stir well. Put on floured pastry cloth and knead until smooth. Roll into a long log. Cut off small portion and roll out on round pastry board.

Grill on round lefse grill (is there another shape?) at highest heat.

Cover with cloth, wax paper, and plastic to keep in the moisture.

Aunt Dorothy, one of several Ourens carrying on the oatmeal lefse tradition, recommends using one cup of oatmeal rather than the original half cup. She also says, "The oatmeal

Lefse-making demonstrators from Story City, Iowa, at Vesterheim, the Norwegian-American Museum, Decorah, Iowa

flakes tend to make dry spots which are less 'stretchy.' I first put oatmeal in the heated liquid to sort of 'pre-cook' it more. This makes fewer 'holes' when I roll it out."

No matter the ingredients, lefse is best served warm: buttered, sugared, and rolled up like a rug! *Vær så god!*

Vær så god, literally meaning "be so good," is a common Nordic expression used before meals which means "come to the table."

Recommended Nordic Menu for Lutheran Church Dinners

LEFSE plus LUTEFISK plus red JELLO

Note: Lutefisk is dried cod. The traditional preparation involves soaking the fish in a lye solution for two or three days, then cooking it in salt water. It can be purchased today needing only to be rinsed and cooked in the salt water.

Fisk, Glorious *Fisk*

By Robin Ouren

Somebody has to do it. Someone has to peddle lutefisk. Mike Field of Mike's Lutefisk Company in Glenwood, Minnesota, is among the few who make a living catering to the weakness of helpless Norwegians.

Mike is not Norwegian. He isn't even Scandinavian! He admits this freely, saying, "I'm a little bit of English, a little Irish, a little German, and a little Bohemian." None-the-less, he lures in countless *fisk* addicts.

Mike has been in the lutefisk business for over twenty years, starting out in the town of Brooten, Minnesota, fifteen miles south of Glenwood. There, he bought a grocery store, and learned that the previous proprietor made lutefisk for his customers. So Mike tried it himself. The store blossomed. Eventually, Mike and a friend put up a building in Glenwood. There, Mike sells lutefisk, lefse, and pickled herring. But mostly lutefisk.

How much lutefisk? Four-hundred-thousand pounds per year! Mike sells retail and also wholesale, throughout the United States and in Canada, to Scandinavian Festivals, Sons of Norway, and many churches — no doubt Lutheran. "I sell to *Høstfest* (Annual Norwegian Festival) in Minot, North Dakota," says Mike. "We use three tons for that dinner."

Mike is not alone in his mission to distribute lutefisk. In addition to Mike's company, there are three other companies in the United States that do so. New Day Fisheries is in Washington state, others are located in Minnesota: the Day Fish Company is in Braham, and the Olsen Fish Company, recognized as the largest processor of lutefisk in the world by the Norwegian Stockfish Organization of Bergen, Norway, is in Minneapolis. According to Olsen's "unofficial manager" Roger Dorff, the company sells over half a million pounds of *fisk* each year. Between the four companies, over one million pounds of lutefisk are distributed over the three-hundred-sixty-five-day period! Not surprisingly, church dinners make up a good portion of the buyers. According to Mike, churches go through around three to four thousand pounds for their one-day *fisk* feasts.

Lutefisk does not start out as lutefisk, according to Mike. (A note before we go on: The word "lutefisk" has only two syllables. The *correct* pronunciation is loot-fish. Say that with a Norwegian lilt.) Lutefisk starts out as codfish, swimming happily about in the North Sea or elsewhere off the Scandinavian coast. Norwegian fishermen trick the cod into coming aboard ship, promising them fame and fortune in America. Once on board, the *fisk* realize the ruse and expire from the shock of being lied to. Then the cod is dried on large racks, sorted by size, and exported to the lutefisk shop. "In this dry form," says Mike, "it becomes what they call a stockfish. After it is shipped over here, we go through the process of soaking it out. It takes about twenty days to soak a batch of *fisk* out from start to finish." The *fisk* is put into tanks according to size and soaked in fresh water for about three days. Then, the all-important lye is added. "In a sense, the lye sort of cooks the *fisk*," says Mike. This process takes up to ten days, after which the *fisk* goes through the whitening process, where the lye is rinsed out.

Many people, Norwegians even, don't understand the lutefisk process. This is why Mike offers tours through his plant. Sons of Norway groups and hundreds of others from across the country make the journey to Mike's each year to take the tour and to buy *fisk*.

Though he is not Norwegian, Mike seems to have acquired a nice Norsk accent. About this, he says, "It kind of goes with the territory. If you are around it enough, it gets on you, I guess."

In Defense of Lutefisk

By Robin Ouren

"Save the Whales." "Defend the Dolphins." "Be Kind to Lutefisk." Everyone has to have a cause, and why not campaign for a kinder and gentler treatment for a DEAD species for a change? Only an insightful Norwegian would take up such a cause.

"Be Kind to Lutefisk" could be the anthem for an organization with the lofty goal to educate the world about lutefisk, destroying once and for all the hundreds of jokes surrounding the traditional Norwegian delicacy. Or at least it SHOULD BE! And it would be, if such an organization really did exist.

In researching lutefisk, sifting through recipes and countless jokes, I recalled my own memories of having lutefisk mainly at Christmas, which raised the annual question of my grandmother: "You're soaking it in WHAT!?" I am half Norwegian, but I never could bring myself to taste lutefisk since the smell alone was a close enough encounter. (I have never admitted this before, and now that I have, I feel much less guilty.)

So, while researching and reminiscing, I tried to explain this tangle of sensory perception and shaky loyalty. I was stopped dead in my tracks when I made a few wisecracks about lutefisk to some full-blooded Norsks. Scandinavians, as we have all heard at least a *tusen* (Norwegian for one-thousand) times laugh at themselves. They are secure—comfortable enough with themselves to make light of their customs and traditions.

Tossing out a few jabs at lutefisk, I chuckled at my cleverness and glanced around the room. Steely blue eyes threw looks that only Norwegians could muster. Cold. Hostile, even. The eyes betrayed disapproval and hurt. Norwegian pride. I knew it, and I thought I better run before the Viking sword came off the wall over the fireplace. But I stayed, hoping to learn something I didn't already know about lutefisk so that maybe the gods would be kinder to me when I went to Valhalla, or wherever non-warriors who don't eat lutefisk end up after this life.

I was given only one quiet bit of advice: "Be kind to lutefisk." A hush came over the room at the mention of the great "L" word. I thought I even heard organ music wafting down from the heavens.

Then it dawned on me. Norwegians can take a joke, but lutefisk deserved more respect. After all, lutefisk is the staple of staples in Norway. It could, if necessary, fill most of the basic human needs: food, love, shelter—all those things. As for food, lutefisk has probably pulled many a family through lean times. As to love, everyone has to love SOMETHING, and giving is always better than receiving. Norwegians can love lutefisk for all of its benefits and receive unconditional love in return. Lutefisk never judges, after all. How could it? And, lutefisk can be used to shingle a roof, when other suitable materials (like oatmeal lefse) are not available. Lutefisk by the front door can also serve as protection. What troll would exchange her infant for a human baby and subject it to a lifetime of lutefisk?!

In this country, lutefisk has a cult following. The Norwegian Lutefisk Supper (and Swedes practice this too) is a given occasion in Scandinavian-settled areas. Over a TON of lutefisk is served at the annual lutefisk church dinner in Poulsbo, Washington. Nordic Fest, held in Decorah, Iowa, each July hosts a lutefisk eating contest in which contestants furiously feast on the fish and then place the empty bowls on their heads. One wonders whether serious Norwegians would partake of such an obviously disrespectful event.

What lutefisk really needs is a patron saint. Maybe Saint Torsk, or Saint Fisk. Of course, this would mix Catholicism into a basically Lutheran idea, but it might help lutefisk gain some dignity. Or maybe it just needs more people like me to become sensitive and crusade for its rights. Then I would also have to stop berating it with wisecracks and jokes. Which reminds me of my favorite lutefisk recipe: Place lutefisk on a board. Add salt, pepper and baste with butter. Bake in oven. When done, throw out the fish and eat the board.

There is the old saying about never judging anyone until you have walked a mile in their shoes. If this applies to lutefisk, then I suppose it is time I tried the stuff—then I can lambaste it with a clear conscience. Be kind to lutefisk? This "Ultimate Norwegian Joke" is more popular now than ever, and it is so because of the supposed "bad press" it gets on T-shirts, bumper stickers, and out of the mouths of good-natured Norskies. Why be kind? Lutefisk has a long history, a huge following, and because it, too, is Norwegian, it can take a joke or two.

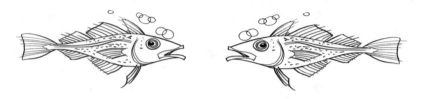

Of Loons, Of Lutefisk, Of Folklore

By Donna Lee

Excerpts from *The Providence Journal-Bulletin*, Rhode Island

Many Swedes and Norwegians from Minnesota flee winter to vacation in south Texas, so when I visit relatives in Texas I'm as likely to get Norwegain flatbread from their friends as I am to get enchiladas at a Mexican restaurant.

At a party during one visit, two Norwegian-Americans entertained by singing "O Lutefisk," pronounced "lude-a-fisk," to the tune of "O Tannenbaum"—spoofing the malodorous fermented fish that Scandinavians traditionally serve at Christmas.

I asked, "If lutefisk is so awful, why do you eat it?"

"We love it! It's traditional," said one of the women. "But it smells so bad that we can't bring any with us on the plane."

Fortunately, there are plenty of other Scandinavian dishes with more general appeal, such as a recipe for Troll Pudding called "Things That Go Bump in the Night." The first ingredient is "1 quart cream, not too fresh."

A Scandinavian newsletter includes proverbs, such as this from the Finns: "When you hear the call of the loon, stay off the ice." (Makes sense. If the loon is back, the lake must be thawing.)

In Poulsbo
It's Lutefisk by the Ton!

By Dana Lumby
Information from Earl Hanson

Thousands of pounds of lutefisk, thousands of people and eighty-three years is what the Annual Lutefisk Dinner is all about. Reminiscent of Norway, the little town of Poulsbo, Washington, is home to this world-famous dinner.

In 1913, the Fordefjord Lutheran Church (now known as First Lutheran Church) first pulled the lye off the shelves, poured it on the codfish and opened its doors to the public.

Each year on the third Saturday in October, more than 1,000 people participate in the feast, during which over 600 pounds of potatoes, 1,300 pounds of lutefisk, 3 large boxes of apples, 100 pounds of cabbage, 300 pounds of meatballs and gravy, and 1,900 lefse are consumed.

For the record, the greatest amount of lutefisk served at one of the annual dinners was 2,200 pounds. "Sometimes you have to get a wheelbarrow to wheel out the lutefisk," said Earl Hanson. One year, they ran out of lutefisk. What did they do? "Well, we fed them **meatballs**," says Earl.

Rolling meatballs

*Poulsbo Queen Lisa Jorgenson and her court
helped serve the 1995 dinner.*

The church crew in Poulsbo purchases lutefisk by the truck-load from New Day Fisheries in Washington state. New Day prepares the lutefisk and delivers it to the church in their refrigerated truck. The church crew then cooks the *fisk*.

At this annual feast, expect the following menu: Lutefisk, Norwegian Meatballs, Boiled Potatoes, Potato Lefse, Special Lutefisk Dinner Salad, Sliced Fresh Tomatoes, Home-baked Cakes, Coffee (lots of it), Tea, and Milk.

When Queen Sonja and King Harald V of Norway visited

Poulsbo in 1995, Earl Hanson, Sons of Norway cultural director, escorted them through town. King Harald commented that Poulsbo reminded him of Norway. A parkway bears the name of King Olav V, King Harald's father, who fell in love with the city when he visited in 1975.

Making lefse

This "ode to lutefisk" is sung to the tune of "Oh Christmas Tree" by Washington state trolley conductor, Eldo Kanikkegerg, around Christmas time. It has been reported to be heard in Texas too!

O Lutefisk!

This Norwegian Loves You!

O Lutefisk, O Lutefisk, how fragrant your aroma!
O Lutefisk, O Lutefisk, you put me in a coma!
You smell so strong, you look like glue!
You taste yust like an overshoe!
But Lutefisk, come Saturday
I tink I eat you anyvay.

O Lutefisk, O Lutefisk, I put you by the doorway!
I wanted you to ripen up yust like they do in Norvay!
A dog came by and sprinkled you,
I hit him with an army shoe!
O Lutefisk, now I suppose,
I'll eat you as I hold my nose.

O Lutefisk, O Lutefisk, how vell I do remember,
On Christmas Eve how we'd receive our big treat of December.
It wasn't turkey or fried ham,
It wasn't even pickled spam,
My mother knew there was no risk,
In serving buttered lutefisk.

O Lutefisk, O Lutefisk, now everyone discovers
That lutefisk and lefse makes Norvegians better lovers.
Now all the vorld can have a ball.
You're better than that Geritol,
O Lutefisk with brennevin,
You make me feel like young again.

Westby, Wisconsin

49

The Washington Prairie Lutheran Church, Decorah, Iowa,
hosted a dinner at the annual Nordic Fest.

I Remember
Christmas and Lutefisk

By Bengt G. Johnson

To the Scandinavians, it was almost a religious rite—to eat lutefisk on Christmas Eve. My parents had to have it and my sisters and I, much as we dislike it, had to eat it too! But we survived.

About December first, the fish market on 7th Street would lean huge slabs of this lye soaked, dried codfish or ling, outside the store-front just below the display windows. Pedestrians walking by would splash winter slush on the slabs. But worst of all would be stray dogs; let's just say that the dogs were comfortable displaying their lack of affection for the delicacy, lutefisk.

Until my father died at the age of forty-seven, we ate this glop every Christmas. But when I became head of the house, things changed. I informed my mother that there would be no more lutefisk, no more salt pork and no more mashed turnips. She agreed. All went well until the following Christmas.

About mid-December, I attended a stag party with a few of my friends. To get in, everyone had to pay a dollar for a chance on a turkey. The crowded room reeked of tobacco smoke. Several poker games were noisy with money changing hands at the turn of a card. But the loudest cries came from the two crap tables where the entreaties of the player mingled with the clatter of the dice against the side board.

In the midst of the stag party revelry, I was announced as the winner of the turkey!

As the days of Christmas neared, I presented my claim ticket for the turkey at a local meat store. The bird was huge — twenty-two pounds! At home we found that it wouldn't fit into our oven. The only solution was Schrom's Bakery. They agreed to stuff, roast it and make gravy. We all looked forward to a glorious Christmas Eve meal, but my Uncle Albin stopped in late that afternoon and cast a pall over our plans.

51

He and my Aunt Nannie wanted us all to come for supper on Christmas Eve — the day the bird was to be ready. Mother and I decided that we would have the turkey on Christmas day, because Nannie would probably serve ham.

December 24th came. I picked up the turkey in the morning. It came hot and brown from the huge oven and had a mouth watering fragrance. All day long its aroma wafted through the house. Late that afternoon, on the way to Uncle's house, we tried to divert our minds from the turkey by talking about the nice baked ham Nannie would probably be serving.

What did she serve? Lutefisk with boiled potatoes and green peas! I've never forgotten that night, and it has been fifty-six years!

Lutefisk Tasting Day

By Julie Ingebretson

Lutefisk Tasting Day began in 1991 as part of the 70th Anniversary celebration of Ingebretsen's Scandinavian market-place in Minneapolis. So much fun was had that it is now an annual event.

Small portions of the "stuff" (just a few bites, or slurps) are served with plenty of butter—this arouses either love or hate, not much in between!

The first year, a running tally of "thumbs up or thumbs down" was scored by a few locally prominent lutefisk experts, including former Minnesota governor Wendell Anderson. The result: 98 percent, "Lutefisk is wonderful!"—2 percent, "Lutefisk is terrible!" Not exactly a scientific survey, but who wants to be scientific about lutefisk?

Succeeding tastings have been held without the scoring and celebrity intervention, but other features have been added—live music; hilarious guest "celebrities," such as Tim Furlong, who invented the lutefisk fishing lure, and day-long sales of lutefisk merchandise such as T-shirts. Wildly creative ideas are brewed up for each "tasting" event. Regardless of the itinerary, it's a blast!

Lutefisk Eating Contest

Nordic Fest photographs by
Joan Liffring-Zug Bourret.

Nordic Fest, Decorah, Iowa

ontestants are each given a bowl of lutefisk. The first to place the empty bowl on his
her head is the WINNER!

Annual Nordic Fest Parade
Decorah, Iowa

OLE'S LIES
TRAVE

WE'RE GOING TO THE OLYMPICS,
"JUST FOR THE SPORT OF IT"
O MY COD, ISN'T THIS
LILLEHAMMAR?

SHOCKS
BRAKES

FLY SNOOSE AIRLINE

DESIGNED & BUILT BY THE
BRIGHT Brothers FROM
IGNORANT Coo

PAUL'S
ELECTRIC RAZOR
SERVICE

TOUR NORWAY $49.50
SEPT 31
SNOOSE AIRLINE

Queen Helmi Drag Contest for St. Urho's mate

Finland, Minnesota

St. Urho

Gregory Kellerman, Queen, right, with his court: Aaron T. Wilson, James P. Stevens, David Jokela.

Photographs by John Johnson & Joan Liffring-Zug Bourre

Finnish Fun
The Truth About
St. Urho

By Richard L. *(Lovable)* Mattson

Winters are long and cold in Virginia, Minnesota, on the Iron Range. Gene McCavic, a co-worker at Ketola's Department Store, chided me in 1953 that the Finns did not have saints like St. Patrick. I told her the Irish aren't the only ones with great saints. She asked me to name one for the Finns.

So I fabricated a story and thought of St. Eero (Eric), St. Jussi (John), and St. Urho. Urho, a common Finnish name, had a more commanding sound. So I said, "We have St. Urho. To save the grape crop, he drove the poisonous frogs from Finland before the last ice age."

The women decided to have a St. Urho party in Ketola's coffee room. They made a cake with purple and green frosting. Mrs. McCavic wrote this poem in her "Finglish" dialect:

Ode to St. Urho

Ooksie kooksie coo ana veee vee
Sainta Urho iss ta poy for me!
He sase outa rogs so pig unt kreen

Praffest Finn I effer seen!

Some celebrate for Saint Pat unt hiss nakes
Putt Urho poyka got what it takes.
He got tall unt trong, um feelia sour
Unt ate culla moyak effery hour.
That's why tat guy could soot tose rogs
What crew as pig as chack bine logs.
So let's giff aa cheer in hower pest way
On May dwenny fort, Saint Urho's tay.

Boast ript: Kiitos Rhikku, for delling us ta histree off tis Zooperman Urho.
Da main vloor kitts.

Clarence W. Ivonen of the *Mesabi Daily News* soon featured the birth of this new saint in, of all places, a department store. The folk legend of St. Urho grew; others embellished the original poem and wrote their own versions.

Through the years, I have given lectures proclaiming this Saint lost in antiquity. I have explained many times to rapt audiences that he was born of peasant stock on the Finnish-Swedish border. After showing promise in schools, he was given a scholarship to a Stockholm seminary, and studied in Paris under the humanist Catholic theologians.

When Urho returned to Sweden, he was given a parish in a rural area. There he was constricted and felt he had more to give. Since he knew the language, he was transferred to Southern Finland, where farmers grow crops of barley and oats. A small creek and bogs created an ideal breeding ground for poison frogs. When oats and barley had tender shoots, the frogs massed and crawled over the shoots, leaving the poison secreted from their skins which had a devastating effect on the new young crops. The people appealed to the Kalevala Gods and then to the Christian Gods with no results. In desperation, they asked their new priest, Good Father Urho, to help them.

After studying the problem, and the height of a frog jump, he built a sluice by a meadow along the stream. He made the sides high enough to keep the frogs inside to eventually go to a holding pond. The frogs were sailed to France with ice in the hold of ships to preserve them. Thanks to the Finns, this is how the French first acquired their taste for frog legs.

There is only one problem. Finland has never had a grape crop. While the Kalevala, the national Finnish epic poem, mentions poisonous toads, I thought frogs would be more appealing.

There is also a story about how Winston Churchill was inspired by St. Urho. When a reporter for the London Times in his youth, Churchill covered Finland, its land and peoples. While in Samiland (Lapland), he marveled at the beauty of the northland and upon leaving noted the Sami people made a "V" sign as they were taught to do by St. Urho. Churchill's interpreter told him the fingers in a "V" meant "Peace to you." Later

58

during World War II, when he needed a rallying symbol for England, he remembered up with the "V" sign and made it a Victory sign.

Originally St. Urho's Day was to be a May celebration, but everyone wanted to have the party in March as the Finnish answer to St. Patrick! The response became phenomenal—going nationwide within a few years with programs, parades, parties, greeting cards and buttons. I have heard there is a movement in the southwestern states to make St. Urho the patron saint of refrigeration, which makes it possible to ship fresh fruits and vegetables to the rest of the nation. Who knows when and where miracles will end?

A letter to the editor in the *Finnish American Reporter* states: "Back in the days before he was a saint, Urho was known to occasionally lose his temper. One time when he was dipping a fish net into a tank of lutefisk, the bottom of the net was eaten away by lye. In his anger, Urho hurled the net across the room and it stuck in a crack in the wall. Still angry, he flung a piece of flat rye bread in the same direction. Much to his delight, the flat bread banged off the wall, went through the net, and rolled back to him. He decided to make a game of it, which he called 'bread-kit ball,' which naturally evolved into basketball."

As the legend grew, a professor of psychology, Sulo Havumaki, in 1958 at Bemidji State, changed St. Urho's history from frogs to grasshoppers. And grasshoppers it has been ever since.

Columnist Jim Kloubuchar of the *Minneapolis Star* wrote that "St. Patrick merely drove the snakes out of Ireland working a shrewd trade-off with the future settlers of America, who took the snakes and residual rights to 'My Wild Irish Rose.' St. Urho had no such patsies. Working strictly on his own and without benefit of press agents or flit guns, St. Urho drove the grasshoppers out of Finland. He thus saved the Finnish grape crop, without which thousands of Swedes and Norwegians would have died of thirst."

Two statues of St. Urho were created with logs and chain saws at Menagha and Finland, Minnesota. The Menagha Urho is a thirteen-foot statue of the Saint with a giant grasshopper

*Richard Mattson visits St. Urho's Pub in Helsinki, Finland,
as shown in this photo taken by his daughter.*

impaled on a pitchfork. A spaghetti dinner reportedly honored
the Saint. Purple doughnuts made an appearance in New York
Mills. Hugh Mellin of New York Mills, Minnesota, claimed to
have found the Saint's burial site near there. Joseph Kyllonen,
according to a newspaper account, is credited for the governors
of every state proclaiming March 16 as St. Urho's Day.

A book, *Outside Finns* (*Ulkosuomalaisia*) published in Finland
about Finns who live in other countries, featured St. Urho, the
living legend. Ritva Paavolainen wrote the essay after we cor-
responded.

While in Finland in the late 1980s, I visited St. Urho's Pub, a
workingman's bar, close to the Parliament building. There were
three silhouettes of monks in the front windows. I was astound-
ed and continue to be amazed as St. Urho Day is celebrated
decades later at parties and festivities
throughout America with people wearing
green for grasshoppers and purple for grapes.

Richard L. "Lovable" Mattson
Saint Creator

By Joan Liffring-Zug Bourret

Richard L. "Lovable" Mattson

Born on July 4, 1913, Richard is a third generation Finnish American who grew up on the Iron Range at Virginia, Minnesota. The Finnish family surname, Porspakka, was changed when Richard's grandfather worked as a fisherman on the Great Lakes and others called him Matt Mattson. Richard's father worked as an electrician for a sawmill, then opened a hardware store in Finn Town, and later became a partner of the Ketola Department Store in Virginia. Richard worked for his father and eventually managed the main floor of the Ketola Department Store for forty years.

Richard attributes a talent for performance and his love of a good time to his mother Hannah. Participation in local theatrical and singing groups attested to a particular creativity which blossomed in a most unpredictable and unique fashion.

In 1953, Richard created Saint Urho...

...a remarkable feat for a Minnesotan and a Lutheran Finn who is not a Pope. Richard says, "I am proud of St. Urho. Finnish pride is like *sisu*. When they build a log cabin it is perfect. They keep fish nets repaired and they bath regularly in saunas. Bathing in Finland and Finnish America is a ritual. It is not just to get clean, although that comes with it.

"I hope St. Urho will live on. A lot of saints and great men have been forgotten. Many saints have been condemned."

61

1996 St. Urho Celebration, Menagha, Minnesota, King John Matthews and Queen Elsie Veit are shown with official crown of grapes on their hats. Statue of St. Urho, in the background, features a grasshopper, symbolic of the grasshoppers the Saint drove out of Finland in order to save the grape crop.

The Sauna
Finland's Gift to the World

Illustration by David Fitzsimmons from
the book, *Finn Fun*, by Bernhard Hillila

My First Sauna Experience!

From Stop and Smell the Cedars, *by Tony Jellich, edited by C.J. Swanson, an "insider's" diary of Tony's experiences as a longstanding member of the "Men in Gray," or the legendary conservation warden force of Wisconsin.*

After my (game warden) training program at Wisconsin Rapids, I was sent home. My supervisor Kelly Jones said, "Hang around, somebody will probably die from over indulging over the Christmas holidays and we'll put you back to work."

Wouldn't you know it, the legendary Douglas County warden, James T. McNaughton, passed away December 24th. It was a sad day for all the people who knew Jim. Before Jim was buried, I received a call to report to the Superior station to fill in the game warden position.

I obtained a map of Douglas County and began to check the road systems. On a Sunday morning, with the air temperatures fifteen to twenty below zero, I began a trek to look over State Highway 13, which runs along the northern part of the county and just east of Superior.

I had been informed by both the sheriff and police chief that Highway 13 County was "Finn Country" and Finns were not fond of game wardens. The sheriff had said something to me that struck my funny bone. He said, "Be careful that one of those fair-haired Finlander girls won't get you in a sauna." I had never heard of a sauna so he explained the finer points.

Driving down the highway, I saw a pack of dogs pursuing a huge black and white bull, snapping between his legs. I wasn't about to stop and get out to scare the dogs off, so I drove to the nearest farmhouse to report the incident. There were three to four cars in the yard. I tooted my horn a couple of times and out of a small square log building came four middle-aged men, seemingly intoxicated.

They laughed when I told them the story about the dogs and bull. Then, they asked if I would like to have a sauna. "Hell yes!" I said. "How do you go about taking this sauna bath?" They showed me the process. The building had two rooms. One was a dressing room, and the other had a huge stove with a box of rocks on top of the stove. The people were throwing dippers of cold water on the hot rocks. This caused a cloud of hot steam.

I followed directions, and with a small towel, went in for my bath. Jeez, in a minute, I damn near passed out. But it felt good, and after awhile I followed their example and slapped my body with cedar boughs. They passed a jug of vodka around. "Not for me," I said. Shortly, they left.

I began to enjoy it. After twenty minutes I decided to douse myself with cold water as they did. Then out into the dressing room I went. Jeez! All my clothes were gone! I had only that little towel, but my winter boots were still there. I put them on and with my towel, I ran to my car. They had locked the doors and left the keys on the seat. But, I carried a couple keys stashed under the hood and luckily in the late 1940s the hoods could not be locked. For a moment, I thought I was saved, but all I had in the car was a pair of gloves. I headed back to Superior to the sheriff's office.

The sheriff's office was about eight steps up. When you're up there you can look out the window right into a car.

I blew my horn and about ten people came to the window. They were looking directly down at me, all laughing! I kept blowing the horn until Sheriff Ekroth came out grinning. Under his arm was a gunny sack with my clothes. He said, "Those Finlanders dropped off your clothes, said you forgot them after you had your sauna."

Well, over a period of years, I got the names of those who were involved in the sauna incident. It all worked out OK, as I arrested four of the five names for illegal gill netting in the Grule River, deer shining, and transporting loaded rifles.

As Judge Cooper would say, "Everybody pays for education in this great life of chance."

Garrison Keillor

Photograph by Charles Langton

*Garrison Keillor, with Norwegian-bachelor twins,
Aaron and Arvid Swenson of Flom, Minnesota*

Garrison Keillor introduced bachelor Norwegian farmers and Scandinavian "Wobegoners" to a national audience. Keillor portrays Scandinavians with humor and love; thanks to him we can imagine the trials and tribulations of Nordic Lutheran immigrants. Keillor creates fantasy out of local realities.

He was born in 1942 in Anoka, Minnesota, today a suburban area of the Twin Cities. At age 18, he began his career in radio while a student at the University of Minnesota. After graduating in 1966, Keillor's prose was accepted by *New Yorker* magazine. A 1974 *New Yorker* article about the Grand Ole Opry led to his creating for radio "A Prairie Home Companion," for which he received a Peabody Award, an Edward R. Murrow Award and a medal from the American Academy of Arts and Letters. Today, "A Prairie Home Companion" is heard on over 350 public radio stations by almost two million listeners. Keillor is noted as a writer and even as a symphony orchestra performer as well as a one man performance artist. His recording of *Lake Wobegon Days* has earned a Grammy Award, two Ace Awards for television, and induction into the Radio Hall of Fame. "Lake Wobegon Tonight" even performed in London.

The Finn Who Would Not Take a Sauna

By Garrison Keillor

In northeast Minnesota, what they call the Iron Range,
Where men are men and that is that and some things never
change;
Where winter stays nine months a year, there is no spring or
fall
And it's so cold the mercury cannot be seen at all,
Where you and I, we normal folks, would shiver, shake and
chatter
And if we used an outhouse, we would grow an extra bladder.
But even when it's coldest, when *our* feet would have no
feeling,
Those Iron Rangers get dressed up and go out snowmobiling
Out across the frozen land and make a couple stops
At Gino's Lounge and Rudy's Bar for whiskey, beer and
schnapps,
And then they go into a shack that's filled with boiling rocks,
That's hot enough to sterilize an Iron Ranger's socks.
They sit there till they steam out every sin and every foible,
Then they jump into a frozen lake and claim that it's enjoible.
But there was one, a shy young man, and although he was
Finnish,
The joys of winter had, for him, long started to diminish.
He was a Finn, the only Finn, who would not take a sauna.
"It isn't that I can't," he said. "I simply do not wanna."
And so he stayed close by a stove for nine months of the year,
Because he was so sensitive to change of temperature.
His friends said, "Come on, Toivo! Let's go out to Sunfish
Lake,
A Finn who don't take saunas? Why, there must be some
mistake."
But Toivo said, "There's no mistake. I know that I would
freeze
In water colder than myself (98.6 degrees)."

To jump into a frozen lake is not my fondest wish,
For just because I am a Finn, don't mean that I'm a fish."

One night he went to Eveleth to attend the Miners Ball
(If you have not danced in Eveleth, you've never danced at
  all).
And he met a Finnish beauty there who turned his head
  around.
She was broad of beam and when she danced, she shook the
  frozen ground.
She took that shy young man in hand and swept him off his
  feet;
She bounced him up and down until he learned the polka
  beat.
She was strong as any man, she was as fair as she was wide,
And when the dance was over, he asked her to be his bride.
She looked him over carefully. She said, "You're kind of thin,
But you must have some courage if it's true you are a Finn.
I ain't particular 'bout men. I am no prima donna,
But I would never marry one who would not take a sauna."

They got into her pick-up, and down the road they drove,
And fifteen minutes later they were stoking up the stove.
She had a flask of whiskey, they had a couple toots,
And went into the shack and got into their birthday suits.
She steamed him and she boiled him until his skin was red,
She poured it on until his brains were boiling in his head,
To improve his circulation and soften up his hide,
She got a couple birch boughs and she beat him till he cried,
"O couldn't you just love me now? O don't you think you
  can?"
She said, "It's time to go outside and show you are a man."

Straightway because he loved her so he thought his heart
  would break
He jumped right up and out the door and ran down to the
  lake,
And though he paused a moment when he saw the lake was
  frozen

And tried to think just which snowbank his love had put his
   clothes in,
When he thought of his love, he did not have to think twice,
He just picked up his frozen feet and raced across the ice,
And coming to the hole that they had cut there with an axe,
Putting common sense aside, ignoring all the facts,
He leaped! O what a leap! And as he dove below the surface,
It thrilled him to his very soul—and also made him nurface.
And it wasn't just the tingling cold he felt in every limb,
He cried: "My love! I'm finished! I forgot I cannot swim!"
She fished him out and stood him up and gave him an
   embrace
That warmed his very heart and made the blood rush to his
   face.
"I love you, darling dear," she cried. "I love you with all my
   might."
And she drove him to Biwabik and he married her that night.
And they live happily to this day, although they sometimes
   quarrel,
And there, I guess, the story ends, except for this: the moral.
Marriage, friends, is not a banquet; love is no free lunch.
You cannot dabble around the edge, but each must take the
   plunge.
Though marriage, like that frozen lake, may sometimes make
   us colder,
It has its pleasures too, as you may find out when you're
   older.

Finland has a million saunas.

The phases of a sauna are: 1. Perspiration
                             2. Beating with a birch whisk
                             3. Steam
                             4. Washing
                             5. Rinsing
                             6. Cooling off
                             7. Air drying
                             8. Rest & Refreshments
                                (coffee, juice, beer and sausage)

Imported immigrant troll,
Høstfest, *Minot, North Dakota*

Beginner's Guide to Trolls

By Robin Ouren

Most people are familiar with the folk tale *The Three Billy Goats Gruff*. This story is a Norwegian creation, and tells how three billy goats outsmart a troll who lives under a bridge. The bridge troll, called *brotrollet* in Norsk, is one of many trolls that hover in the shadows, waiting to surprise, scare, and sometimes even eat an unsuspecting human who may wander by his or her lair.

You may have thought that trolls were mythical creatures created by Norwegians hundreds of years ago, but that is not so. Trolls are real—at least in the hearts and minds of everyone who has heard the tales over and over again as they were handed down from generation to generation.

Trolls live everywhere, from under the sea to high up on mountain tops. They come in various shapes and sizes, from the huge *jotul,* or giant, to the tiny *marmel* who can easily fit inside a mitten. Trolls can be male or female, they can have one or many heads, always have tails, and are never clean. Often, moss, dirt, and other unpleasant things grow on them, making them even more difficult to see. Sometimes, trolls' noses are so long and so covered with dirt that trees grow out of them (next time you are walking in the woods, remember to walk lightly, for you may, in fact, be trodding over a troll's head). Trolls are also not very bright, which is why the three billy goats were able to outsmart the one that lived under the bridge.

The most popular troll—the one that has become Americanized over the years, is called the *nisse* (pronounced NIH-seh). The *nisse* is the Norwegian and Danish equivalent (called *tomte* in Swedish) of the word goblin, but you are probably more familiar with the terms gnome or elf. These creatures are the ones that you see wearing the little red caps and looking cute as they sit on people's shelves or in their windows. But the *nisser*, too, are trolls. And, rather than living out in the woods, they set up housekeeping in people's houses and barns, playing pranks on the animals and the people who live there. (The *nisse's* favorite places are the kitchen, the attic, and the hayloft.) Whenever there is trouble in a Norwegian home—something mysteriously gets knocked over, the cows get out, the bread in the oven fails to rise—one suspects that the *nisse* has been around.

Legend has it that the *nisse* is really the person who originally owned the land, clearing the timbers and building the house and farm. Many believe that the original owner—even long after his death—returns to the land to make sure the place is being taken care of. And while he visits, he expects to be treated with hospitality, or else he will cause trouble. This is why many people set out a bowl of porridge with a dab of butter in it on Christmas Eve. They hope to appease the *nisse* so that they might have a year with very little mischief. Sometimes it works!

Despite their bad reputation, however, *nisser* and other trolls continue to co-exist with humans, and we are the better for it. Whether you are Scandinavian or not, the troll tales provide us with many opportunities to pass on stories to our children, just as the troll tales were handed down to us. And, a *nisse* watching over one's house from the mantle or a shelf can add much to our days. For without a little unexplained mischief, without a little fear of the unknown, life wouldn't be quite the same.

On the "Troll Trail," at Norskedalen, the Norwegian Valley Nature and Heritage Center of the University of Wisconsin-La Crosse Foundation near Coon Valley, Wisconsin.

Vinnie Nelson, Knife River, Minnesota, and a little creature with reindeer fur from Samiland that came to her by twists of fate. After it was
rescued from a truck carrying it to the Red Wing "dump," its new
owner's dog was terrified of this troll-like being. Threatened with
abandonment, it was given to Winnie. They are shown here enhancing
the jewelry display of her son B. E. Nelson, a silversmith, at the
Høstfest in Minot, North Dakota.

With waffles on his horns, wearing the colors of Sweden, Dave Nohling promotes Vasa Lodge #349 Viljan foo booth at the Scandinavian Day Picni Vasa Park, South Elgin, Illinois.

Authentic Viking Reenactment

(No horns!!)

L. to R.: Gary A. Anderson, Derr Anderlick, and "Magnus Hrolf," who is wearing his politically correct "roadkill" fur at Vasa Park.

Big Ole

Alexandria, Minnesota

ALEXANDRIA
BIRTHPLACE OF
AMERICA

Cousin Byron Gunderson of
Glenwood, Minnesota, waves from
the base of "Big Ole." This "Viking"
has a winged helmet.

The Big Ole

By Robin Ouren

Standing "big" in the street near the Runestone Museum in Alexandria, Minnesota, is a Viking statue known as Big Ole. How big is Ole? Twenty eight feet tall and weighing in at four tons.

Big Ole was built by Gorden Displays of Minneapolis for the New York World's Fair in 1965. The statue was to be part of an exhibit which would include the famed Kensington Runestone and the story of the Viking explorers who allegedly left it behind. The theme for the fair's Minnesota Pavillion was "Minnesota, Birthplace of America."

The fair opened on April 21, 1965, and in two days' time, more than 250,000 people viewed the exhibit and Big Ole. After the fair, Ole was moved to Alexandria. Borrowing a little thunder from the nearby hamlet of Kensington, where the runestone was actually discovered, Ole's shield proudly announces Alexandria as the "Birthplace of America."

Endangered Species

In 1967, Ole had a close call. The Santa suit he sported for the Christmas holiday caught fire. Three thousand dollars later, he was repaired. Ole has been repainted twice, and in 1991, also got a new hair color. His original gray hair and beard were replaced by blonde locks, in keeping with ideas of Scandinavian explorers, or maybe just so he could feel more like his twenty-six years. He was moved once from a busy inter-section, to avoid being hit by cars.

Big Ole is probably in more family photo albums than he cares to admit. Every year, thousands of tourists stop in Alexandria to have their picture taken next to him.

The Kensington Stone
Runestone Museum
Alexandria, Minnesota

By John Zug and Robin Ouren

It was 1898, in Kensington, where a midwestern mystery of epic proportions began. A small Scandinavian-settled town in the west central part of Minnesota, Kensington is home of the Runic Stone, possibly dating back to the year 1362.

According to records, the stone was discovered by Swedish farmer Olof Ohman, who was clearing trees in a field a few miles north of Kensington. He discovered a stone slab, tangled in the roots of an aspen stump, approximately thirty inches high, sixteen inches wide, six inches thick, weighing in at around two-hundred pounds. A cryptic message was carved on the front and one side of the stone.

Upon sending a copy of the mysterious writing to a Swedish-American newspaper in Minneapolis, it was learned that the message was runic, meaning the runic alphabet consisting of 24 angular characters used by Scandinavians, as well as Anglo Saxons, for inscriptions and secret writings from the third to thirteenth centuries.

The deciphered message told about eight Swedes and twenty-two Norwegians on an exploration from Vinland in the year 1362—one hundred and thirty years before Columbus "discovered" the continent. The message described how the group was camped by a lake, and after some of the party returned from a day's fishing, discovered ten of the men massacred. A prayer to the Virgin Mary followed the account.

The Kensington stone received much attention, but no one could declare its authority. Ohman then proceeded to use it as a step to his granary for nine years!

In 1907, Hjalmar Holand, a University of Wisconsin graduate, with a passion for Viking history, visited Ohman and took the stone with him for further study. He made it his life's work to prove the authenticity of the stone and fulfill his desire to prove the Vikings explored America beyond the northeast coast.

In 1928, Holand sold the stone for two-thousand dollars to businessmen in Alexandria, Minnesota. Throughout the 30s, the stone traveled around in the back of a touring car, driven by Lorayne Larson, daughter of one of the Alexandria businessmen. Lorayne Larson, who soon came to be known as the "Runestone Girl," gave lectures throughout the country about the stone's discovery.

A Runestone Museum was built to house the stone, which became a permanent part of Alexandria. Many other artifacts were found in the area surrounding Kensington, some authentic, others yet to be proved.

Those interested in making a trek to the actual site of the stone's discovery may travel south to rural Kensington. At the crest of a hill in Runestone Park, four flags, honoring the United States, Sweden, Norway and Minnesota, stand by a monument to the runestone. Just down the hill is a second monument on the actual discovery site.

The book *"The Kensington Runestone Vindicated,"* by Rolf M. Nilsestuen, published in 1994, summarizes the controversy that has raged over the authenticity of the stone. Nilsestuen, a scientist, points out significant pieces of evidence that help to verify the authenticity of the stone—medieval documents and practical matters related to the discovery. Robert A. Hall, Jr., Professor Emeritus of Linguistics at Cornell University, writes: "The burden of proof now rests on the 'negators'…to refute the large body of evidence that proves the inscription is genuine and to show how and by whom it could have been forged."

If a hoax, the Kensington Runestone was an elaborate ruse which has put the towns of Kensington and Alexandria on the map. If authentic, it has proved that the Viking explorers traveled to Minnesota, the real "Birthplace of America."

About the

Vikings

By John Zug

A history of the Vikings would tell of people living in what is now Norway, Sweden, and Denmark. Writing, if it had been available, would have recorded the people's stories of the beginnings of the earth, and of the gods, and of the peoples—how they built to protect against attack from the mountains or from the sea—how they adapted to a climate of short summers and long winters, and how they buried their dead.

By the time the written word arrived, Christianity had pushed forward from the south, labeling many of the north-land stories and ceremonies with the derogatory word "pagan." Generations later, some of the stories of the Vikings were learned from artifacts and from writings of the literate monks in raided monasteries.

And then there are the myths, born anew today as in the past. The dark eyes of an occasional Norwegian conjure up dreams of Viking ancestors wintering in the Mediterranean; the rare blue eyes among Native Americans hint of Old Norsk of the Viking era who were on the North American continent hundreds of years before Columbus sailed the ocean blue.

The decline of the Roman Empire after 400 A.D. gradually caused Roman troops to be moved south out of Europe. These troops had been the foundation of such law and order as existed. Thus began the thousand sad years of the Middle Ages, when people became serfs (slaves), bound to the land claimed by their owner, whose life, in turn, was no safer than the strength of his castle, which was his fort.

Education was in danger of dying out; it was rare for anyone outside the monasteries to be able to read and write. Robber gangs were everywhere, and there was no law or police force to stop them. There were hundreds of castles. When one changed hands, whether by force, or as a result of a marriage, or whatever, all of its land and all of its serfs became the property of the new master. Children born of serfs were the property of the master.

Into such a society came the Vikings from the North. The Vikings created superior ships—swift, with beautiful lines, suited for relatively shallow rivers, yet seaworthy. The years of the Vikings were from about 750 A.D. to 1100 A.D. It has been written that the Roman soldiers had kept out "the barbarians of the north." There was no one to stop the Vikings when they came from the north by sea. The Vikings attacked monasteries—some of which were rich—and villages, and brought home slaves as well as loot and precious metals. The era of the Vikings ended only as defenses against them were built.

It has been difficult for later peoples to explain the Vikings. The Vikings have been called seagoing, but this hardly fits the people who opened trade routes through Poland, southerly through all of Russia, and onward to Byzantine, which became Constantinople and now is Istanbul. Vikings have been defined as marauders in search of plunder and slaves, but this hardly explains Old Norsk colonizing efforts in Scotland, Britain, Ireland, Iceland, and Greenland, not to mention the leaving of their calling cards on the North American continent. Vikings have been called pirates, but pirates battled the ships of governments for their gold, and governments were few and weak in the days of the Vikings.

Normandy, a province on the English Channel in northwest France, is named for the Northmen who settled it in the 800s and 900s. In 1066, William I, Duke of Normandy, became William the Conquerer by crossing the channel into England with an army and winning the battle of Hastings from the troops of Harald II, who rushed south but were weary from repelling an attack from other Northmen. Descendants of William I have been kings and queens of England ever since.

In A.D. 800, Pope Leo III crowned the great Charlemagne Emperor of the Romans. Charlemagne, King of the Franks, conquered most of Europe. He and his successors helped push Christianity steadily northward, eventually dooming much slavery, promoting law and order, and eventually reaching the Scandinavian areas of the various Vikings.

It took a long time to take up where the Romans left off, and many traditions have their origins in the Middle Ages. Among these colorful traditions, some are dead serious, and none are more fun that those of the Vikings, **even if the Vikings of old didn't sport the horns of today.**

Out of this background came the pleasant and fun traditions of the modern-day Vikings. The word signifies alertness and happiness, whether it is the name of a football team, a Scandinavian get-together, or a school party. The costumes are festive and, yes, today's Vikings like what they do, whether the goal is victory, fellowship, food, or fun.

The Dilemma of the Horns

Vikings wore no horns
By Dennis L. Johnson, *Nordstjernan,* Oct. 5, 1995

Since helmets with horns on them appear whenever there is any vaguely Viking-ish event, *Nordstjernan* decided to pursue this question once and for all. Margareta Talerman at the American Swedish Historical Museum in Philadelphia was happy to help kill the myth of those horned helmets.

All Viking helmets found in archaeological digs have been "hornless," according to Margaretha Talerman. She adds that whenever there is a Viking exhibition somewhere in the United States, plastic helmets with horns are always on sale in the museum shops. It seems that it is what people want.

Cookie jar made by Dakota Stoneware Pottery, White, South Dakota

Magnus Hrolf

Founder of Viking Age Club of Chicago

You will find him at dozens of Scandinavian festivals, parades and events in the Midwest, but you won't find his name in the phone book. Magnus Hrolf is a professional Viking impersonator. This historian Viking buff, who has taken it upon himself to re-educate the public about the life of the Vikings and ancient Scandinavian traditions, remains incognito.

After researching his own Nordic genealogy, Magnus determined that much of the history of the Viking Era was misleading—emphasizing only the battles and destruction by the Viking pirates. Subsequently, with facts in hand, he began his mission to bring to light the civility of the Old Norse society—the importance of the ancient farmers and their strong family values honoring women and children.

In 1994, he founded "Ancient Norsk Games," recreating the Old Norsk means of developing life skills in a fun way that attracts children as well as adults. Magnus appears as a grand figure in full Viking garb, including jewelry and battle gear, when he participates in these reenactments. He is quick to point out that any costume bearing fur is strictly "roadkill," a modern-day Viking code of conduct!

He has devised and distributes a Viking Code of Conduct, emphasizing loyalty, honor, industry and achievement as individuals and as family. Included in these principles are: *"Don't be greedy." "Don't get drunk." "No shame in going to bed early." "Treat women as equals in all rights."*

Magnus reports that one woman cried with joy and thanked him for dispelling the negative myths of her Viking ancestors. He considers this a just reward!

His appearances, geared to all ages and understanding of the old, wise Norse, include: lodges, schools, festivals, parades, encampments, and other events. He continues to research and write Viking Era articles for newspapers and newsletters.

Note: Magnus Hrolf is pictured in full Viking regalia on page 75.

Leif Ericson Society
"BeLeifers"

Information from Ivar Christensen
Leif Ericson Society International

Evidence of the stalwart inclination toward exploration and discovery by the Vikings is embodied in the goals of the Leif Ericson Society International. First started in 1926 as the Leif Eriksen [sic] Association of Philadelphia, the group faded into almost nonexistence until 1970 when Ivar Christensen of Media, Pennsylvania, put the pieces together to build an organization that is now 999 members strong. (Membership is held there since Norwegians have trouble pronouncing "th.") Mr. Christensen says, "We are serious about our goal: to get Leif Ericson as much credit for showing the way as others have received for following it! However, we inject a touch of humor from time to time...For a dollar you can get on the waiting list. It is a long list! For $25,000 a member can have dinner with the president [me]. That sure beats Clinton's offer! For $50 a member can have a McDonald extravaganza with the lookout on the Viking ship 'Norseman.' Actually that translates to $150 for a life membership; $10 annual minimum dues; $1 for clergy."

The Society makes a significant contribution to expanding knowledge about the rich Nordic-American heritage and history of the American continent. Notably, they commissioned research that polled a sample of 212 history department heads from U.S. colleges and universities to determine once and for all who was the first explorer to set foot on the shores of North America. Unaided, 39% agreed that Leif Ericson was the first; 72% agreed that it was a Viking or Norseman; only 5% agreed that Christopher Columbus was first. Promoting "Leif Ericson Day" on October 9 each year, as proclaimed by Congress in 1964, is ongoing along with maintaining the spectacular Viking ship "Norseman." Newsletters, press releases, and events keep members and the public informed.

The "BeLeifers" are true-to-Nordic—they're serious about working for their purpose, but they have fun doing it!

Leif Ericson Viking Ship(s)

The Ravnen

A notice in the newspaper read: "If you don't buy this ship, we'll burn it." It continued: "Know anyone in the market for a good used Viking ship that was owned by a little old Norsewoman who only took it on raiding parties every other Sunday? Better yet, know anybody interested in buying a Viking fixer-upper vessel?" Any takers were to contact the Leif Ericson Viking Ship Association because they were having a hard time finding a buyer for the "Ravnen," a 30-foot replica of a Viking longboat that was christened in 1976 as the Leif Ericson Viking Ship. Retired from sailing in 1988, after years of taking part in parades, launchings, exhibits, and voyages, the "Ravnen" succumbed to age, dry rot, and a collision with a Buick while being towed to a parade.

Then President of the Leif Ericson Society International, Ivar Christensen, noted that "if there were no buyers...they may have to junk her....We are thinking of setting it adrift down the Schuylkill and putting a torch to it in the old Viking style. In the old days, a dead Viking chieftain was buried with it. But I'm not ready to go yet, and we don't have any candidates at this time."

The story of the "Ravnen" has a happier ending! Almost fairy-tale-like, Emma Schachner of Swarthmore, Pennsylvania, wished for a Viking ship for her tenth birthday, and she got her wish! She and her seven-year-old sister, Sarah, were both interested in early explorers, especially Vikings. Their father, Bob, showed them the notice about the Viking boat for sale. The two girls raided their piggy banks and found a grand total of $128. Getting in touch with the Leif Ericson Viking Ship arm of the Society, the Schachner's negotiated and the boat was theirs.

Their mother, Jude, confessed to a "sinking" feeling the day the boat was to be moored in their back yard. The reality—a 30-foot boat with a dragon's head on its prow, a scrolled tail in the stern, a red and white striped sail with a black raven, and twelve round Viking shields on its sides—was just sinking in. What about the neighbors? The craft was welcomed with awe by Sarah and Emma, along with a crowd of neighborhood children and adults. The "Ravnen" was an instant success, providing hours and hours of imaginary play and educational fun.

The Norseman

Sometime before the final disposition of the "Ravnen," plans were underway to build a new, seaworthy Viking ship that would be in New York Harbor in 1992, for the 500th Anniversary of Columbus' first voyage to the West Indies. (Fun)draising, through individual contributions and sales of "Leif Landed First" merchandise, made it possible for the 36-foot "Norseman" to make its first major appearance in New York Harbor on July 4, 1992, as part of the "OpSail '92 Parade of Tall Ships." Skipper Marty Martinson said: "We had the shortest tall ship in the parade, but we led the historic division, since the 'Norseman' was a replica of the earliest ship. She is a most seaworthy and stable ship, an attribute, no doubt, traceable to the Viking ancestry of her hull design."

The Leif Ericson Viking Ship Association, a separate nonprofit organization, oversees maintenance, scheduling appearances, outfitting and providing the crew of "weekend" sailors, who come from all corners and careers.

Weekend Viking Warriors

While having a lot of fun as "Weekend Viking Warriors," the group is dead serious about its mission. Appearances of the "Norseman" play a large part in the educational purposes of the Society. "We are dedicated to replacing the year 1492 with the year 1003 in the minds of all America's school children and adults," said Gene Martenson, past president of the Leif Ericson Viking Ship Association.

Fulfilling a full schedule, the "Norseman" carries this message with dramatic Viking verve. On Leif Eriksen Day, celebrated in Philadelphia on October 9, onlookers may see the ship cruising or encrouched on the banks of the Schuylkill River, manned by a crew in full Viking regalia—fur-clad, bearded, horned-helmets—with an air of plunder and pillage. But not these "Vikings," they disembark to join in the events and to prove that Leif Eriksen did indeed discover the Americas in 1003.

Celebration in 2003

From "Turning Over an Old Leif…"
By Dennis L. Johnson, *Nordstjernan*, Oct. 5, 1995

The Leif Ericson Society's mission to educate the public about early Norse journeys to the New World is ongoing. Plans are underway for the Leif Ericson millennium celebration in the year 2003.

Society members regularly challenge (often tongue-in-cheek) public actions which slight the discoveries of Leif Ericson. Members say that when Columbus raised a glass with the first Native American chief that he met and said "Salute!" the native chief responded with a loud "Skol!"

Opposite page: "Viking Ships" 1897 *by*
Erik Werenskiold. Courtesy of Vesterheim,
Norwegian-American Museum.

The Longship Company
Viking Ships

The Longship Company of Maryland, another educational organization, operates mainly in the Chesapeake Bay and tributaries. They boast the 32-foot "Fyrdraca" and the 20-foot "Gyrfalcon." The company organizes cruises, races, historical pageants, research voyages, living history encampments, waterfront festivals, lectures, special construction projects, museum tours and demonstrations, and...

...burning Annapolis to the water line.

A June 1992 article in the *Washington Post* reported that "these Vikings...rowed their dragon-headed longship up to the City Dock (Annapolis), grabbed their axes and broadswords, and clanked around town in chain mail and armor. If that was not scary enough, their captain let it be known that his name is 'Atli' which comes from 'Attila,'as in the 'Hun.' The warriors had put out a press release that their activities would include: 'dock walloping' and 'burning Annapolis to the water line.'"

This voyage was prompted by the impending visit to Annapolis of the Nina, Pinta and Santa Maria, re-creations of Columbus's fleet. The "Fyrdraca" docked a day before their arrival!

"Once again, we got here before you did," Atli said to the man portraying Christopher Columbus, when the two great navigators met in the parking lot. The commander of the Columbus fleet asked, "What are you?"

The short answer reported by the *Post* was **"Hell's Angels of the 10th century."** The long answer was: "a Maryland based group of medieval enthusiasts....Although his forbears' names have become practically synonymous with the words 'rape and pillage,' Atli comes across more like Mister Rogers than Hagar the Horrible." The threats of "walloping" and "burning" smoldered to the headline: **"Oh, Those Silly Vikings!"**

Medieval Reenactments
"bashing stress"

In the same spirit of Viking voyages, medieval reenactment groups abound. With similar enthusiasm, these groups seek to replicate in costume and custom the world of 10th-century Vikings. Dramatic role-playing creates a time warp in which Viking combat in full armor—hacking away with impunity—is a socially acceptable creative outlet for stress and aggression!

"Lay On!"

All in the name of fun and history, Vikings of these recreation groups pair off and exchange lusty blows. There is a method to their madness. Members research roles and abide by rules set by the *thynge* (or *ting*), an assembly modeled after medieval hierarchies of law and justice. Rules are essential in the heat of battle, some of the rules that apply: If you are hit above the knee, you lose the use of that leg. The same goes for arms. A direct head shot is a kill. Everything from the wrist to fingertips and below the knee is an illegal blow. When these Vikings drop a shield or a metal legging becomes unclasped, they are not instantly dead. With a cry of "Hold!" all fighting stops and equipment is adjusted. A shout of "Lay on!" resumes the contest. No warrior is allowed on the field if he is angry or upset. One member states: "The whole idea is to go out, do some bashing, not get hurt and have a lot of fun."

A set of armor can weigh as much as sixty pounds. It's not unusual for contestants to sweat off several pounds in a summertime battle. This leads one to reason that the Vikings usually fought either early in the day or late in the day to avoid the worst heat—death from heat prostration was every bit as serious as death by the sword. The dead of winter is considered "fine fighting weather"—for Viking pretenders, that is!

An ideal battleground is found at Slippery Rock, Pennsylvania, where there is an historical reproduction of a castle. The warriors split into two opposing forces, and the hills come alive with the sounds of battering rams downing the castle door, swords crashing on shields, the ground literally shaking.

Following these, often Oscar deserving (some die better than others) performances, rivals gather to share a jug of mead, and a little less vigorous form of partying.

Forging History

Some groups have their own "smiths" that forge the armor, but the business of "Arms and Armour," located in Bouse, Arizona, is to replicate weapons and armor as nearly authentic as possible.

"Bahadur Design" of Sequim, Washington, focuses mainly on jewelry, but has created many custom designs for Medieval recreationists.

From the Bayeux Tapestry, showing drinking horns and bowls similar to those found at Viking sites   From *Proverbs from the North: Words of Wisdom from the Vikings*

Vikings Invade Georgetown, Texas

Information from Irma Pearson

The Vikings have a long history of invasions—from continent to continent, across perilous seas—leaving behind a sense of awe at the powerful Scandinavians. Today, the Vikings have "invaded" once more. Texans experienced, first hand, the Viking experience. Not to fear—these Vikings arrived to show an estimated 15,000 Texans how to party.

These present day Vikings arrived in station wagons, in sports cars, and spectacularly by boat. The "Norseman," a replica in the style of the 9th-century Viking ship of explorer Leif Ericson when he crossed the Atlantic to the New World, was anchored in the San Gabriel River at Georgetown, Texas, and led the way for the celebrations to begin. The colorfully bedecked "Norseman" was complete with crew members dressed as Vikings. Hauled by trailer to Texas, at night flood lights illuminated the dragonhead, and strings of lights outlined the hull of the proud ship with its red and white flag flying. Festivites began with *"ankomst parad,"* with dancers and musicians coming up from the ship at river's edge.

"The Viking Fest," the first Scandinavian immigration celebration of its kind in Texas, was held in April of 1996. Sponsored by VASA (Swedish-Scandinavian cultural organization), this gathering celebrated the 100th Anniversary of the founding of VASA, and the 150th Anniversary of the first mass immigration of Scandinavians to America. An estimated crowd of 15,000 came to unite their efforts in the preservation of Scandinavian heritage in America.

Twenty Nordic clubs from around the state were represented. Consuls and national anthems represented Sweden, Norway, Finland, Iceland and Denmark. The opening event drew an estimated crowd of 9,000 along with TV personalities, and greetings from Georgetown Mayor Leo Wood.

Texas Vikings wear horns.

Heritage Exhibit Hall in Georgetown displayed materials of importance to Nordic Texans. Extravaganzas of entertainment were presented on two large stages. The days were complete with exhibits, games, art and craft vendors, food, "Viking" goods, special games for children, a chocolate wheel, tombola, and a drawing for SAS tickets to Scandinavia. The Society for Creative Anachronism, of San Antonio, set up a traders' camp with period furnishings, actors costumed in tunics and animal skins, drinking out of horns, and performances of old Nordic ballads and songs. Sword fights were re-enacted in a twenty-foot Nordic tent.

Scandinavian communities from throughout Texas participated with displays portraying their history and culture. These included: Clifton, the Norwegian capital of Texas; Danevang, the Danish settlement; New Sweden; Palm Valley; Type; Ericksdahl's stone church on the Plains, and McCulloch County's East Sweden.

The festival, spearheaded by Irma Pearson (VASA's Grand Lodge Deputy, Central Region) as a VASA project, started out to be a picnic in the park! With the cooperation of the three VASA Lodges and other Scandinavian groups comprising the Viking Fest Board, the festival grew into a statewide event.

Folk Art and Traditions

World's largest Dala Horse and this Dala Clock are in Mora, Minnesota.

John Johnson photographs

A "Rock Troll" guards a candy factory in Sweden.

Mary Lou Hattery photograph

"Hi! I'm a Troll. What are you?"
Allen Bakke (left) designed this 1500-pound PARADE TROLI who lives on Bakke's farm near Elbow Lake, Minnesota. Stee rods and wire mesh hold him together. Lyle Alvstad of nearb Ashby applied a covering of stucco. Note belly button sign.

Greetings from TrollOdin!

Wood cut-out trolls, Ole and Lena shown above, right, are by Bernetta, done exclusively for Open House Imports, on the Trollway of Mount Horeb, Wisconsin. Waving is live TrollOdin surrounded by latex immigrant trolls. Wood carvings, at left, are trolls by Eric Ouren, Waterville, Iowa.

Julebukker, from Spring
Grove, Houston, and Caledoni
Minnesota, are shown "fooling
the Valdres House on the grour
Vesterheim, the Norwegian-An
Museum in Decorah, Iowa. Bui
Valdres, Norway, 1795, this typ
small farmhouse was moved to
museum site and restored in 19

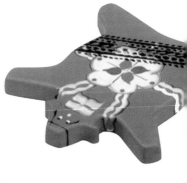

Flattened
Wooden Norsk Dala Horse, with tire
tracks, from an anonymous collector of
Norwegian-American trivia, who is
searching for a Dala Horse, seated.

Here We *Gå Julebukk*

By Robin Ouren

Scandinavians have a great sense of humor. This is because they have been initiated through the old custom known as *Julebukk* or "Christmas Fooling."

The term *Julebukk* means "Christmas goat" and dates back hundreds of years to pre-Christian times in Scandinavian countries. In those days, people had many unusual beliefs. People thought that the *Julebukk* lived in the forest during the year, and as the winter solstice neared, the goat began creeping toward the house. Each day, the goat came closer until it reached the house on the darkest day of the year.

With the arrival of Christianity, the custom was celebrated on Christmas Eve. There, the *Julebukk* hovered in the shadows, waiting to grab unsuspecting children who dared stray from the firelight. Christmas porridge (some believed it was beer the goat was after) was set out for the goat, and, once the goat had its fill of the porridge, or beer—and a few kids for roughage—it left. If there was no porridge, goat havoc ensued in the form of furniture breaking and general frightening of the inhabitants.

Over time, an unusual custom known as *Julebukk* was derived from such beliefs. *Julebukk* involved dressing up in animal skins and goat masks, and carrying goat heads on poles. Costumed participants roamed through the neighborhood yelling and carrying on in an attempt to scare away the ghosts and evil spirits that haunted during the dark winter months. Later on, the goat idea faded, and people simply dressed in masks and old clothes.

Participants gathered together in their garb sometime between Christmas and Epiphany, and set out for the houses of neighbors. As they neared farmhouses, *julebukker* would yell and knock on windows to alert the inhabitants of their arrival. This was followed by barging through the front door and demanding that the family guess their identities. If no one could, then food and drink were demanded. Goat vandalism was generally left for the folk stories.

Often times, once all identities were guessed and the goodies were consumed, the inhabitants donned masks and costumes and joined the group of *julebukker* proceeding onward to the next house. The group's eventual destination was a house party with dancing and singing and more Christmas goodies.

The *Julebukk* practice still continues in Norway, and in America in Scandinavian-settled areas such as Decorah, Iowa, and Spring Grove, Minnesota. To Norwegians, all of these activities are considered socially acceptable, desirable, and good old-fashioned fun.

There is a real art to *Julebukk*, as participants try to disguise their identities with limps, humps, padded stomachs, and strange voices. Masks vary from simple paper sacks or nylons to more elaborate papier-mâché animal heads and other varieties. It takes skill to guess the identities, too. And, of course, one must have a great sense of humor to be awakened from sleep at eleven p.m. by loud and obnoxious uninvited visitors who look like they belong on *Star Trek*, and who demand coffee and spirits and what is left of the Christmas baking before they leave.

Warning

This custom does not do well in big cities. In Chicago, people with nylons over their heads who walk through front doors tend to get shot. Scandinavians in these places just have to forego this type of holiday fun, or else wait until Halloween. No, this custom is good only in small communities where people know it is going to happen, and look forward each year to *julebukker* tramping snow all over their living room and interrupting Perry Como's Christmas show.

Julebukk is a yearly social event, but it also serves to initiate and welcome new members to the community. Or to help them decide if they really want to stay.

"Foolish Memories"

By Robin Ouren

Gladys Tolander grew up in rural northeast Iowa, just a few miles east of Waterville, the town where she has lived for the past fifty years. For Gladys and her family and friends, *Julebukk* or "Christmas Fooling" played an important part of Christmas season festivities, providing social contact and strengthening ties in the community.

Gladys is a "Christmas Fool" from way back. She became a part of this yearly custom in the second decade of this century, and remembers well: "It was sort of a tradition with the Scandinavian people. They did it in Norway especially. I probably started when I was fourteen. That would be about the youngest that went. We usually went out between Christmas and New Years, but you know, a lot of times, it would be way out in January. We would buy masks and keep them from one year to the other. They were cloth with paint on them so they were stiff. A lot of times you just painted your face, but sometimes this was not enough to disguise oneself from the neighbors.

"Some of them," says Gladys, "would have a crazy hat on, and the men a lot of times would dress in a long dress. Some women dressed as men, some didn't. Some had actions that showed more when you put pants on, and you could see your actions a little too close. They'd put wool scarves over their heads when it was cold. You usually tried to get a scarf that people hadn't seen because sometimes they'd know your clothes. Of course, you'd disguise your voice.

"Once dressed, the 'fools' would trek out into the neighborhood. We would walk, or sometimes we'd take a car, but cars had to be left far enough away so they would not be recognized. The groups were different. There were all the way from five or six to maybe fifteen. Then there were those who went along—Irish even—because it was fun. And it was.

"Upon arrival, the fools would make noise and, altering

their voices, shout 'Christmas Fools, Christmas Fools.' Most people expected the visitors, and so, inhabitants would open their doors, welcoming the 'fools' and offering food and drink while attempting to identify their visitors. They tried to guess. They tried to pull our masks off.

"Most of the time it was hard for us to eat because we had that mask. We had to be careful, because they'd try to see you when you'd open your mask. If they did guess who you were, you took your mask off."

Sometimes, residents joined the group and the lot proceeded on to the next house. The fools made the rounds to five or six houses, and occasionally ended up at someone's house to play cards.

Christmas Fooling could be hazardous too. Gladys remembers going out with friends and family members one night when the snow was deep and crisp enough to walk across the top. "I wore Uncle Olaf's wedding suit and we went Christmas fooling to some of the neighbors," she says.

While attempting to cross a barbed wire fence, Uncle Olaf, not exactly a spring chicken, slipped and went to the ground. "I didn't more than help Uncle Olaf up near the fence post and the first thing I knew, my feet went out from under me and I sat down!" recalls Gladys. "Oh, Uncle Olaf laughed. I can just hear him laughing yet."

For Gladys, Christmas Fooling stopped after she was married and started her own family. "By that time," she says, "it kind of died out, along with many other ethnic traditions in America." But, she remembers those days fondly. "It was good-hearted" she says, "we had a lot of fun."

Illustration by David Fitzsimmons

You can always tell
A Norwegian...

By Robin Ouren

It is true. You can always tell a Norwegian from anyone else, including all of the other so-called Scandinavians.

To begin with, there is the unmistakable accent. Though this is less common in younger Norwegians, it is a telltale sign of Norskness among the over-sixty group. There are two pronunciation rules to remember. The combination "th" is pronounced as "t," and "j" must sound like "y." An example of this would be: "Jumpin' Jehosaphat, it's my thirty-third birthday! I guess I'm not a youth anymore!" Pronounced as: "Yumpin Yehosaphat, it's my tirty-tird birtday! I guess I'm not a yoot anymore!"

This leads directly to Norwegian phrases. Not known for lengthy exposition, Norwegians have to include vocal variety in few syllables. For example, "ja" is the Norwegian word for "yes." Variations on "yes" abound. Ja, sure. Ja, you bet. Ja, you betcha. Ja sure, you bet. Ja, that's it you know. "Uff da" is, of course, a staple in the true Norwegian vocabulary. The phrases too, are more prevalent among older Norskies, although many teens do use them. Their unfortunate American pronunciation just tends to make it more difficult to discern their heritage.

A more reliable sign among younger Norwegians is food preference. Norskies eat things like lefse and lutefisk and krumkake, particularly around Christmas. If you don't know what any of these things are and still wish to find a true Norwegian, simply look at the color of the meal. "White meals" are common with Norwegians. Potatoes, meats such as fish or chicken, a slice of bread next to the plate, milk mush, and a glass of milk on the side. Three or more of these items at a meal is a good indication that you have discovered a Norwegian.

A real Norwegian listens to the incidental music from "*Peer Gynt*" the epic play written in 1867 by Norway's native son Henrik Ibsen (1828-1906). Norwegian composer Edvard Grieg

(1843-1907) wrote the incidental music for the production.

Did you hear that Ole loved Lena so much, he almost told her? True Norwegians tend to be on the quiet and unexpressive side. Of course, this characteristic is sometimes hard to discern among males, where it often crosses ethnic borders. The quietness combined with a strong constitution and the determined yet sad look of a true stoic leads one to suspect that he has stumbled onto a Norwegian.

All of this leads to a sure sign of a true Norwegian—the infamous bridge bump. We are talking here about the unmistakable hump that the bridge of the Norwegian nose sports. This bridge bump pegs a Norwegian without a shadow of a doubt. Simply stand to the side of a person so you can get a look at the profile. The Norsk nose is a slope with a convex protrusion in the middle that even a Telemarker would hesitate to ski across. When all else fails, this simple "nose test," will tell you, "That's Norwegian."

Eric Ouren, holding one of his troll carvings, displays a striking Norwegian profile.

Letter by a Norwegian Immigrant

This letter, handed down in my family, is by my great-grandmother who defied her father to marry my Swiss ancestor John Lang. They left Gunder and Elgin, Iowa, immediately after the wedding ceremony for a honeymoon in a covered wagon headed west. She had a happy life raising two sons on a farm in Plymouth County, Iowa. Only one of her sisters, married to a Lutheran minister in the Dakotas, kept in close touch with her. Her eldest brother Sven died serving the North in the Civil War. She named her youngest son Samuel, anglicizing Sven. Gunhild and John made a trip in the 1890s to their ancestral homes in Norway and Switzerland. Now, 150 years later, my 100 percent Norwegian cousins are finding me, including third cousin Joyce **Sullivan** of Seattle, Washington.

—Joan Liffring-Zug Bourret, publisher

Le Mars, Iowa
April 8, 1873

Dear Cousin Tom Enerson,
After my long delay, I now take my pen to answer your letter. I see by your letter that you are in good health, and I greet you with the same greeting that we are in good health at the time of this writing.
We are wondering if any of you will come to visit us? Maybe you would not care to come for my husband and his brother are German. **My husband is a good man, just as good as though he were Norwegian.** That is what I have experienced or learned. He is a remarkable and good man.
One of his brothers is staying with us and he will soon marry a Swede girl. I am very happy about that because it will be more company for me. **Being a Swede, that is as good as Norwegian.**

Gunhild Gunderson
(Nellie Lang)

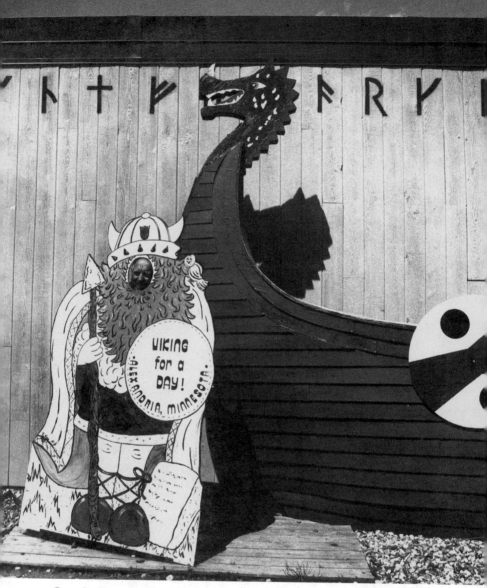

Cousin Byron Gunderson, of Glenwood, Minnesota, grandnephew of
Gunhild Gunderson is the face in this "Viking" cut-out at the
Runestone Museum, Alexandria, Minnesota. Cousin Byron is seen,
also, posted by "Big Ole." Norwegian Americans are fanatical ama-
teur genealogists! Byron is Joan Liffring-Zug Bourret's second
cousin, once removed.

104

The Funny Pages

By Robin Ouren

Scandinavians are everywhere in America. Turn to the comic section of just about any newspaper and you will see "Hagar the Horrible," the little Viking himself. Bearded, helmeted, and wielding a sword, Hagar was created by Dik Browne and son Chris Browne. Hagar's life and times can be seen also in more than thirty books. Browne has won the "Reuben Award"—the highest honor given by the National Cartoonist Society—not once, but twice. So far!

Hagar the Horrible lives the typical Viking life: pillaging with the boys, contending with lousy weather, and enduring on-going marital struggles. Hagar shares the strip with friends Helga, Honu, Hamlet, Snert, Kvack, and sidekick, Lucky Eddie.

Hagar is not the only comic strip with a Scandinavian flavor. *"Han Ola og han Per,"* is one from the past. Per and Ola appeared in the *Decorah Posten,* Norwegian newspaper, from 1918 to 1935.

Per and Ola typified the many Norwegian immigrants struggling to adapt to American ways. The strip, created by Peter J. Rosendahl, represented the rural community of Spring Grove, Minnesota, Rosendahl's home and the oldest Norwegian settlement in the state. Rosendahl had no formal training in art, and learned cartooning through correspondence study.

Per and Ola underwent tests and trials with new-fangled inventions such as the automobile, contended with farm animal mishaps, and got themselves into a lot of foolish situations. There was also an element of escapism in the strip, as the pair flew about in their plane, the "Spirit of Decorah," and visited faraway tropical islands or the North Pole. Per's wife Polla, mother-in-law Værmor, and brother Lars also appeared in the strip.

Rosendahl died in 1942. The final *Decorah Posten* was published in 1972, but Per and Ola live on. They can be seen wandering through the streets of Spring Grove, just ahead of the "Hagar the Horrible" float, waving to the homecoming parade crowd once every ten years.

Om "Tail Light" paa Kua About Taillights on the Cow/April 24, 1931

1. "What in the world are you doing, Per?" "Haven't you read in the *Decorah-Posten* about this new law? We have to put taillights on the cattle."

2. "Oh, Værmor, will you please fill some kerosene in the taillights this evening and light them. Ola and I are going to the whist club, and it might turn out to be late for us."

3. "Now, I've lighted the taillights, but it was terrible how bright they got." "Good gracious, Ma, you surely haven't filled them with gasoline?"

tail lights—baklykter
kerosin—paraffin
good gracious—gode gud
gasoline -bensin

This "strip," depicting the antics of these folk heroes of Norwegian-American immigrants, is from the 1988 bilingual edition of More Han Ola og han Per, *edited by Einar Haugen and Joan N. Buckley, published by the University of Iowa Press.*

The Church Lady

By Susan Griffith

Excerpt from *University of Iowa Alumni Magazine.* Autumn 1995

Hellfire and brimstone just aren't Jonna Jensen's style. In fact, this prairie preacher packs nearly as many punch lines as she scripts sermons.

"If being a parish pastor required me to be serious and strict and stern," Jensen says, "well, I'd have to go do something else, 'cause I just don't have it in me."

With a remarkably upbeat and incorrigibly cheerful personality, the thirteen-year veteran of the ministry practices what she preaches. From the pulpit at the United Church of Christ in Central City, Iowa, Jensen expounds God's love through sermons that are peppered with an occasional story rich in Scandinavian humor.

"One of the neat things about Scandinavian humor is that we tell the jokes on ourselves," explains Jensen. "It's a gentle kind of humor in that it's the Norwegians who tell the 'Sven and Ole' stories, and by presenting ourselves as the punchline of our own jokes, we learn not to take ourselves so seriously."

A third-generation Norwegian American, Jensen delights in telling and retelling the tales about Sven and her ancestors. "It's a family racket," she announces with a smile. "We were telling the same one-hundred years ago."

As Jensen speaks, her cherubic face and twinkling eyes become even more animated, and it's soon apparent that the thirty-nine year old reverend laughs as easily as she breathes. With little warning, she launches into her sing-songy Nor-VEE-jun accent.

"Ole is praying, and he says, 'God,'" Jensen begins, "'vy you make my Mrs. Lena so cute? Vy you make her cheeks so rosy? Vy you make her dimples so sweet? Vy you make her dumplings so light? Vy you make her so huggable under da feder bed at night? Vy you make my Lena that way? And God says, 'Yah, Ole, dat's so you vil love her.' And Ole prays some

Reverend Jonna Jensen
Norwegian-American minister with humor

more and says, 'God, vy you make my Lena so pitiful stupid?' and God answers, 'Yah, der Ole, dat's so she vil love you.'"

...Blessed with irrepressible good humor, Jensen regales her parishioners with the decades-old-Norwegian stories in an effort to convince them that life and church are really not such a serious affair.

"When people come to worship on Sunday morning, they've either had a hellacious week, or they're going to have a hellacious week, and they need to have their safety and comfort needs met first," Jensen says. "And you can't start with the holy haranguing until people are feeling safe and welcomed and relaxed.

"People are hurting enough and have enough sense of stress and rejection. You know what it's like by the time you get to Friday night? The last thing you need on Sunday morning is a little more hassle and aggravation."

Although Jensen enjoys every aspect of parish ministry, she's quick to note that it's not always easy to find comic relief in a world that's all too often not very funny. But whether she's preaching to a full house or providing spiritual counseling on an individual basis, her infectious humor helps alleviate anxieties when it comes to discussing some of life's most troublesome concerns.

"You can deal with a lot of difficult issues by using humor," says Jensen. "It kind of takes the edge off. And sometimes we can get places with humor that we couldn't get just whomping people over the head, which isn't pleasant for either one of us."

Ordained a pastor in the United Church of Christ, Jensen heeds a congregational style of government. Based on the assumption that the Holy Spirit resides within each member, denominational authority, in turn, lies with the members. Although Jensen says the lack of directedness is glorious and refreshing and empowering, she also admits that this style of ministry can be very challenging.

"You have to know the Bible, and you have to have some line of prayer relationship with God," she says. "But other than that, you're on your own. It's like we handed you the direction to this thing and said 'work it.'"

"It is exciting, though, and it's a lot more fun for me as a minister to be a companion to people on a journey and to accompany them as they are working out what it is that God is calling them to do." Jensen continues. "You know, I wouldn't last three minutes in the kind of ministry where I say, 'Quit that. You gotta stop that.' I don't like it myself, and it just wouldn't be much fun."

...Each Sunday, Pastor Jonna, as she is fondly referred to, incites the children in the congregation to take center stage for a junior sermon. In a conversational and confiding tone, she offers the kids their own Bible lesson, while the adults watch and listen.

"Rather than thinking church is a place where we bring the children and mold them up to be like us, I think more of what we're about is bringing the children in to look at them and learn from them," she says. "The idea isn't to make them more like us, but to remind us what they're like so we can continue to be as much like them as is humanly possible."

Reminiscing on her own childhood recalls the first stirrings of her call to ministry. Growing up in Maquoketa, Iowa, she used to play church and conduct her own worship services.

"I had a little play church up in my room," Jensen laughs at the memory. "I'd sneak up there on Sunday nights, light a little candle, read a little scripture, and sing a little song. I don't have any siblings, so no one else was being victimized by all this, other than my bears and my dolls. 'Sit here, Barbie, we're having church.'"

Eventually, Jensen outgrew her Barbie and her play church and traded in her juvenile avocation for an adult occupation. After earning a bachelor's degree in religion from the University of Iowa in 1977, she took a few graduate courses at Iowa under the tutelage of Professor George Forell, whom she credits for steering her toward parish ministry.

"Professor Forell and I had one of those holy moments together," says Jensen. "I was sitting in his office, and with his wonderful accent he said, 'You know Jonna, there are two kinds of people in this world, there are book people and there are people people.'

"That was kind of a monument of prophecy in my life in which I experienced my academic advisor confirming my call to move along, get with the people." Forell's comments nudged Jensen to respond to the mystical calling she'd felt through her formative years.

Now, fourteen years after graduating from Andover Newton Theological Seminary in Boston, Massachusetts, Jensen has proven herself to be a credible courier of God's message. Her reputation has spread far beyond the sanctuary of the 127-year-old clapboard church in Central City, Iowa, as her ministry of laughter has caught the attention of people throughout eastern Iowa.

When Jensen isn't behind the pulpit or participating in women's fellowship meetings or planning weddings and the like, you might find her "open miking" at a local comedy club or sharing her Scandinavian humor with members of the community's Chamber of Commerce. Armed with a complete repertoire of squeaky-clean "Sven and Ole" stories, Jensen has taken her show on the road more than once in her crusade to treat folks to the healing gift of comedy.

In 1992, Jensen was one of twelve local semi-finalists for the Jay Leno Comedy Challenge, a competition sponsored by NBC.

More recently, Jensen has given up comedic competition, but she continues to share her wit and wisdom with local civic groups, and she frequently performs her stand-up comedy routines at a wide range of social and professional gatherings. Jensen and her son, Noah, both performed at Camp Courageous, a recreational facility for disabled people near Monticello, Iowa.

"I don't think of doing comedy as something in addition to ministry, but I think of it as an extension," she says. "It's just wonderful to see laughter erupt from people who are struggling with some kind of pain or heartache. It's neat to see them lay their burdens down for awhile and watch them laugh so hard that tears roll from the corners of their eyes.

"If telling jokes isn't the world's greatest hobby, then I don't know what is."

Favorite Stories

Efel and Lars
Einar and Ingeborg

By Reverend Jonna Jensen

Wherever I travel, I always tell the story of Efel Svenson. Efel was a championship tractor-jumping daredevil, famous for trying to jump over forty big bales on his old Allis tractor. His hired man, Little Lars, lined up the bales and put a nice plyboard ramp alongside. Efel hops on old Allis and chugga-chugga-chugs up that plyboard ramp, straight up into the air, over one big bale. Into the second one he crashes. The hay is flying and the smoke is thick. Efel crawls to safety and Little Lars cradles him tenderly in his arms.

Efel says, "Uff da, Lars! What you think happened here?"

Lars answers, "I don't know. I'm just Little Lars, your faithful hired man. You're the great Efel Svenson, championship tractor jumper. But how 'bout tomorrow when we try this, we unhook the plow?"

I tell this story because it captures for me something of the heart of Norwegian humor. It's silly and self-effacing, but more seriously, it reminds us that we are all dragging something along behind. All our back ends drag now and then. We all have a little trouble getting airborne when we need to. We have forty bale days and crash into the second bale more often than we wish. That's when it's time to unhook the plow and lay our burdens down a bit. When we get together and tell all these silly Norwegian jokes, we're just unhooking the plow.

Einar and Ingeborg met in heaven. They fell in love and decided to get married. They went to St. Peter and told him that they wanted a wedding. He told them to come back in fifty years.

Einar said, "But I was ninety-seven when I died. I don't want to wait fifty years."

"Ninety-seven years on earth goes real slow," St. Peter answered. "But fifty years in heaven will pass in a snap. So long! See you in fifty years."

Einar and Ingeborg return fifty years later, really ready to get married.

Again, St. Peter tells them to come back in fifty years.

They come back fifty years later, sincerely ready to get married.

St. Peter tells them to come back in fifty years.

Einar gets steamed. "No way! I waited ninety-seven years on earth and fifty years in heaven and fifty more years in heaven. I don't want to wait no more! We want to get married today!"

St. Peter says, "Look, I'll tell you what I'll do. You come back in fifty years. If we don't have so much as one single minister in heaven by then, I'll marry you myself!"

As a pastor. I love that story. As a pastor married to a lawyer, I was tickled to hear this "amendment" to the story.

St. Peter marries Einar and Ingeborg. They come back three years later and tell him it's not working out and they want a divorce.

"A divorce?" St. Peter asks. "Well, O.K. then, if you're sure that's what you want. But just remember. It took me a hundred and fifty years to get you a minister. There's no telling when I'll find a lawyer!"

Heaven's Problems

Illustration by David Fitzsimmons

More Norse Nonsense

From David Belgum

David Belgum, Norwegian-American Professor Emeritus,
University of Iowa College of Religion, presents these all-time
favorite laughs—spirit lifters!

Lars wanted to go ice fishing, but his friend said he needed some special equipment like an ice chisel. Lars told the clerk at the hardware store he wanted "an ice schisel." He began chipping away at the ice when he heard an eerie voice in the distance saying, "There are no fish there." He moved over about forty feet and began working on another hole in the ice. Again, only closer, "There are no fish there." Then Lars remembered the Sunday School story about the boy Samuel, who asked the third time the voice came, "Is that you Lord?" So Lars said the same; and the answer came back, "No, I'm the watchman at this hockey rink."

Lars and Lena were driving to Minneapolis after their wedding. Tentatively, he put his hand on Lena's knee. In response, she said, "Ja, Lars, we're married now; you can go further than dat." So he drove on to Duluth.

The Norwegians were a little embarrassed about winning so many skiing and skating gold medals since they were the hosts of the Winter Olympics. The king is reported to have said, "Do you suppose they will think we are impolite?"

When I was playing under the kitchen table in a Norwegian country church basement, I heard a woman's angry words about an absent sister of the Ladies Aid. Without actually swearing in the church, the worst she could muster was, "Ja, you know how she is; she made a regular Swede of herself."

Ola and Sven were hauling hay in their old truck. They sold the hay for about the same as they paid for it. Ola said, "Ve shur don't make a lot of money on this job." Sven suggested, "How about if we buy a bigger truck?"

I asked Jens how he had been so successful with his hardware store since he had so little education. He explained, "You see that hammer. I buy it for one dollar, and sell it for four dollars. I figger if I can make a steady four percent profit, I'll come out okay. It's vorked yust fine so far."

"Rollin' Ole," 1989 painted wooden folk art piece
by Paul Wilson from a private collection

A Tradition of Bachelors

By Robin Ouren

Great Uncle Elmer was full-blooded Norwegian. Most of his ninety years were spent working on the northeast Iowa farm settled by his father and mother. Elmer was a Norwegian Bachelor Farmer. Just like his Uncle Albert, and many others before and since. This phenomenon has been happening for centuries and goes way back to the "Old Country." By the "Old Country," I mean just about every country on earth except the United States, but I will focus on Scandinavia.

In Norway, it was customary for the oldest son to inherit the farm and for every other male to be kicked out to fend for himself. It basically came down to the fact that the farms there couldn't sustain more than one family. This is what happens when you live in a country that is more vertical than horizontal. Steep and rocky hillsides may be fine for skiing, but they don't generally bring forth bumper crops, unless you enjoy stone soup.

The remaining sons—the ones kicked from the Nordic nest —had to find their own way. Let's be Seamen! So, they joined the ranks of fishermen. My Swedish great-grandfather Frank Tolander tried this. He ventured out into the blue abyss with an old sea captain who was determined to make him a seaman. Frank threw up on the boat—probably more than once. He vowed never to go to sea again. Immediately following, he jumped on a boat and sailed to America, where he recovered from seasickness, married a nice Swedish girl named Olivia, had three kids—Theodore, Olive, and Wilma—and lived happily ever after—farming.

Many of the bachelors did sail to America to make a go of the only thing they knew how to do, which was? Yes, farming! Some married nice Scandinavian girls, but many others took a vow of bachelorhood. Like Uncle Elmer. After all, it was rather difficult to have much of a social life when you spent most of your time walking behind draft horses and a plow. Or milking cows by hand. Or pitching hay into stacks with a very large fork. The little spare time there was, the bachelors spent "going to town," where they could often be seen standing around together in groups, discussing the farm situation. In a small town near my home in northeast Iowa, a certain street corner has always been known as "Norwegian Corner." It was the meeting place of all those bachelors who came to town "back in the old days."

Today, the bachelor situation is not altogether different. Because of fancy air conditioned tractors—equipped with stereos and refrigerators, and holding nearly six hundred gallons of gas—a man can plow and disk and pick corn in the back two-hundred-and-forty for days on end without once returning home. And in the precious little spare time? The bachelors drive into town and drink coffee together at the local co-op. Lonely bachelors on tractors and in co-ops abound in this country.

Uncle Elmer worked hard. He channeled all his energy into the land he loved, and took pride in his accomplishments, declaring "By Jingo!" when he was pleased with something. Evenings after supper found Elmer in his room, spruced up with a fresh pair of overalls, long-sleeved white cotton shirt, and fiddle under the chin. He refined his tunes and practiced for the many house parties that were held throughout the neighborhood. Another reason, perhaps, he never married. It's hard to dance and pay attention to a sweet young girl while also trying to play the violin. Elmer simply chose to fiddle, rather than fiddle around.

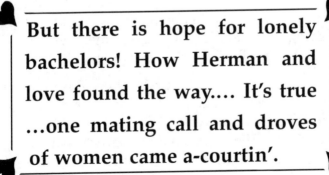

But there is hope for lonely bachelors! How Herman and love found the way.... It's true ...one mating call and droves of women came a-courtin'.

Bachelor Media Blitzkrieg

"The town wasn't sure whether to boast or blush about its lopsided odds—it contained seventy-eight eligible bachelors and only ten marriageable women. Then, one February, Dan Ellison, thirty-seven, a strapping, six-foot bachelor with steady blue eyes and a sweetly shy smile, rose to speak at the annual meeting."   *Good Housekeeping*, January 1995

"Dan Ellison reports that requests for interviews continue. *The Cincinnati Post*, a radio station in Toledo, Ohio, *People Weekly* magazine, *Good Housekeeping* magazine, the *Examiner*, and Minnesota Public Radio are among the media."
                              The Herman Review, Thursday, May, 26, 1994

Also CBS News, the *Minneapolis Tribune*, Oprah Winfrey, Donahue, Sally Jesse Raphael, Leeza Gibbons, The Today Show, and NBC Dateline, just to name a few. And across the ocean too:

"Six months ago, a tiny farming community in Minnesota published an article in its local paper announcing that only ten single women were left living there. Today the writer of that article, like all the other bachelors in the town, receives handfuls of scented letters daily. The biggest concern of the landlady at the Herman Liquor Store Bar is that her clientele of bashful farmers are not taken advantage of by the influx of women. Although Dan [Ellison] talks about economic realities, finding companionship for the seventy-eight bachelors, himself included, was a hidden agenda that he and the others will happily— if a little coyly—admit to. 'If the right person comes along, then I'm not going to say no,' he says with a smile."
                          Marie Claire Magazine (England), October 1994

"Before he got busy on the harvest, Dan Ellison, who works 2,000 acres outside Herman, Minnesota, was actually dating, sometimes three times a week. 'That's a pretty big increase for me,' he chuckles. The bachelorette flood has abated, but some women—fourteen, by Ellison's reckoning—have come to stay."
                                    People Weekly, January 2, 1995

It all started...

Herman needs women! Who is Herman? Not who, but what? Herman is a small town of about 500 people, many of Nordic heritage, located in west central Minnesota. Now it is the most famous bachelor town in the entire world!

It all started in May of 1994, when Dan Ellison—one of seventy-eight bachelors with grim hope for finding true love among the ten available women in Herman—gave a speech on behalf of the Herman Development Corporation. In his speech, Ellison declared, "What we need is more women." It seems that Ellison had been doing some thinking, and determined that the single men to women ratio in the rural community he lived was approximately eight to one. He even went to the local high school and surveyed the young women there. The majority said that they had no plans to stay in the community after graduation. The lack of career opportunities was forcing the fairer sex out of town and creating a community of bachelor farmers.

Ellison believed it was time to do something, like find ways to create jobs for women and attract them to town. He brought these concerns to the board. Little did he know that giving his simple speech would create such a stir!

Within days, the story of his little soliloquy had traveled across the continent. The local newspaper picked it up, and then a local TV station, and then it went nationwide. Suddenly, Ellison's phone was ringing off the hook. Every talk show in the country wanted him! He had to give up farming for a while as he traveled the talk show circuit. On national television, Ellison invited "women of the world" to come to Herman for the One Hundredth Grant County Fair, to be held in July of that year. Sure enough, they came. Women from thirty seven states and five foreign countries descended on Herman. "Bachelor Mania" began. And continues.

The population of Herman is rising steadily. Many of the new residents are women. Several new businesses have been started in town. Three weddings and lots of engagements have also resulted from all of the attention. Ellison is among the lucky bachelors. He met his girlfriend when she bought him at the Grant County Fair Bachelor Slave Auction. He's a happy man.

Many other local bachelors, or "Herman's Hermits" as they were referred to in England, have noted an increase in their social lives. All part of the sacrifice one must make in order to help rebuild the economic base of the community.

Herman is typical of the hundreds of rural communities scattered across the country. Which means there is a goldmine of eligible men sitting out on their tractors waiting to be discovered. Bachelors and Bachelorettes of the world: Unite! If you're looking for love in all the wrong places, try rural America instead. It's a happening place.

"Herman's hermits — a town deserted by women"
Marie Claire Magazine (England), October 1994

"Where the boys are! Tiny town is best place in America to find Mr. Right!"
Examiner, June 1994

"The town that advertised for women"
Good Housekeeping, January 1995

"Where the boys are ... the lonely men of Herman, Minnesota, are hoping to recruit a few good women"
People Weekly, June 20, 1994

"Mating call...When the lovelorn men of Herman, Minnesota, put out the word, droves of women came a-courtin'"
People Weekly, December 26, 1994

Potluck Protocol

By Robin Ouren

It is biting-cold and blustery—a Saturday afternoon in October. Tomorrow, Sunday, is Mission Festival. After the 10:30 a.m. church service, the Ladies' Aid will host a dinner in the church parlor. That is the fancy way of saying "potluck in the basement."

The church is old, made of wood and painted white. The entire upstairs—narthex, nave, and chancel—are light green with dark green carpet and fir flooring underfoot. The altar painting—Jesus standing on the stormy sea and reaching down to save Peter—is a creation of Herbjørn Gausta, the famous Norwegian painter who lived about a hundred years ago. The bell tower still has a real bell. The church sits on a knoll exactly two and a half miles north of Waterville, Iowa. It is, of course, Norwegian Lutheran—East Paint Creek Synod Lutheran Church—member of the Evangelical Lutheran Synod. The Norwegian who named it had a brief lapse into verbosity.

I envision the spread of food at the dinner: scalloped potatoes with ham; the casserole with hamburger, mixed veggies with Tatertots on top; fruit salads, one with mandarin oranges, five or six made with red Jello, fruit cocktail, and whipped cream on top. The red Jello is what I'm bringing. I have to. I'm a Norwegian Lutheran. There will be buns stacked in little baskets, in the center of each of the tables next to the salt and pepper shakers and the miniature mums in milk-glass vases. Emma Dehli, a widowed white-haired farm wife of hardy Norwegian stock, always supplies the mums.

Beverages will consist of water, 2 percent milk and coffee. Nine times more coffee will be served than the other drinks. This is a Norwegian-Lutheran church.

Somewhere in the by-laws of our Synod there must be a section on the protocol of church basement dinners. Why else would the menu remain the same for a hundred years? It is sort of like God. Constant. Trustworthy.

We will gather in the basement, surrounded by white ceiling, walls of tan paneling above, deep brown wainscoting below, and rich wood floors. Pastor Madson, white-haired, spectacled, and in dark suit and tie, will lead the table prayer: "Come, Lord Jesus, be our guest, and with these gifts to us be blessed. Oh, give thanks unto the Lord, for He is good, for His mercy endureth forever. Amen." That is *ah*-men, rather than *aye*-men. It must be thus; for we are Norwegian Lutherans.

The men will go through the food line, heaping their plates as if they aren't allowed seconds. Where they sit will depend on which dessert they like. Desserts are set on the tables beforehand. They will more than likely be next to a relative. This is a small community. Everyone is a relative. A nice feeling, but doesn't do much for conversation. Norwegian Lutherans aren't big on conversation anyway, unless it's about food—or the weather: "Uff da, it's windy out." "Ja, I t'ink you're right."

The women—young mothers along with wizened widows —will stand in the kitchen in little groups, chatting about new dresses, hard frosts and teething babies. They will eye the food counter and rotate the red Jellos to make sure everyone's gets a turn. Once the men and children are situated and appear content, the women will get their plates. Scanning the casseroles and other goodies they will take from the dishes that are the most full — and in smaller portions, wanting to leave food for the hungry, hardy men. Bringing barely-touched food home from a church basement dinner is as shameful as not singing the hymns ("On my heart imprint Thine image, Blessed Jesus, King of Grace!") at the top of their lungs. We have to sing loud. We are...well, you know.

Church-potluck-protocol has spilled over to other denominations. The Swedish Baptists down by Village Creek (an area known to all as Swede Bottom), and some non-Scandinavian-non-Lutherans do things about the same. But they haven't been doing it as long. It's like stepping back in time—traditional roles, traditional foods. Things could be changed, but we take to heart God's words, "I am the Lord. I do not change." And so, everyone seems to be content with things just as they are. We respect tradition. We are Norwegian Lutherans.

How Swede It Is

By Robin Ouren

Meatballs—little round balls of beef, pork, onions and lots of spices are one of the treats Swedes are known for. And though everyone eats them these days, you can tell if an authentic Swede is eating these morsels, or anything else, for that matter. Swedes will be the people eating one course at a time, in the proper order, as in *smörgåsbord* style. None of the heaping-plate mess for a real Swede.

If you walk into a home or Lutheran church basement around Christmas time and are greeted by straw goats of various sizes standing around the rooms or hanging from the tree, you know you are in Swede country. The goat motif goes back to the myth of the god Thor, who rode through the sky in a chariot pulled by two goats. A Swede knows this legend. Straw ornaments depicting stars, angels, and birds are also common on Swedish Christmas trees.

Swedes, unlike their Norwegian neighbors, go to church on Christmas Eve, rather than Christmas Day. For Swedes, the Christmas season is brightened by the custom of Santa Lucia. Santa Lucia (Lucia means "light") was martyred for her faith. According to legend, she returned to earth hundreds of years later to bring food to famine-stricken Sweden. A week before Christmas, Swedish girls dress up as the saint and, wearing crowns of lighted candles on their heads, bring breakfast consisting of buns, cookies and coffee to family members.

Midsommar Fest, celebrated each June throughout Scandinavia and Scandinavian-settled areas in America, is also a bit different for Swedes. If you see dancing around a *Midsommar* pole, and there is not a bonfire, you will know it is a distinctly Swedish celebration.

A Swede knows who Pippi Långstrump (Longstocking) is. Pig-tailed, mismatched-socks Pippi, world-famous literary figure for children and adults alike, is the creation of the beloved

Swedish writer Astrid Lindgren. A Swede would most likely admire Jenny Lind, a nineteenth-century singer, known as the "Swedish Nightingale," who found international fame and inspired an American line of Jenny Lind memorabilia, including clothing, furniture and tobacco products. Movies from the internationally known filmmaker from Sweden, Ingmar Bergman, such as "Fanny and Alexander," could be found in a Swede's video collection.

As for personal characteristics, I grew up with the notion that Swedes were long-suffering, a nice compliment to the quick-tempered Norwegians they tended to marry. I see this within my own family, since my 100 percent Norwegian grandmother married into a 100 percent Swedish family. The Swedes are also very health-conscious, and exercise is an important part of everyday life. No matter how far the destination, it is always within walking distance for a Swede: "You want to go to Helsinki? We'll walk, it's only five or ten minutes."

One thing you won't find in a Swedish home is a Swedish joke book. Unlike those silly Norwegians who insist on churning out self-spoofing books to set on their coffee tables, Swedes have a bit more reserve. You are more likely to find a book of Carl Larsson prints. Swedish painter Carl Larsson is known for his depictions of everyday scenes and life.

Illustration by Carl Larsson used with a poem by his son, Pontius, in a book featuring the work of Carl Larsson (1853–1919).

Lucia and Nobel Laureates

By Anders Neumueller
Excerpted from *Swedish Press*, November 1995

Was it Steinbeck or was it Hemingway? Or was it neither? If you read on, I will give you a scoop.

Every year around Lucia Day, Swedish newspapers tell the story of how the Swedish Lucia had managed to scare a Nobel Laureate in Literature out of his wits. And each year they speculate on which literary giant it was and whether the story is at all true.

All Nobel prize winners stay at Stockholm's Grand Hotel. As the prize ceremonies take place on Alfred Nobel's death day, December 10, the winners also get to experience the Lucia celebration that takes place on December 13.

Many of them have no idea what Lucia is all about, so it is quite a surprise when they are woken up by young voices singing Santa Lucia and white clad maidens serving them coffee and buns. The memory of Lucia with candles in her hair is probably one of the most exotic memories they bring home with them from Sweden.

But for one Nobel Laureate in 1930, the Lucia experience, exotic as it was, was less than pleasant. The American author Sinclair Lewis was a heavy drinker, and it is quite likely that he had had bouts of delirium. We don't know what went through his mind when he was woken up on a dark morning by a white-clad blonde with candles in her hair, and to the sound of a melancholic song about driving out the darkness in the world with light (it was lucky he did not understand the words). What we do know is that Lewis panicked big time. He screamed out and hid his head under the blankets and Lucia and her attendants made a quick retreat.

It was really embarrassing, said my mother. She was the Lucia. Fluent in English, German, and French, she was, at that time, secretary to Mr. Segerstråhle, the legendary head of Grand Hotel. As my mother was also pretty, she was the natural choice for Grand Hotel's Lucia for several years in a row! I still have the books Pearl S. Buck, Eugene O'Neill and John Galsworthy autographed and gave her. But there is nothing in that collection from Sinclair Lewis.

Whenever the story is told in Swedish papers, it is reported to have taken place quite recently, and the victim is believed to be either Ernest Hemingway (1954) or John Steinbeck (1962). But you know that it took place already in 1930.

Illustration by David Fitzsimmons

Lucia and Nobel Laureate

It's Not Easy Being Swede

By Gail Carlson Mackay
Vancouver, British Columbia, Canada

Considering that the Vikings settled in Canada over a thousand years ago (exclaiming, when they landed, "Ja! What a great place for a smörgåsbord—did anyone remember the lingonberries?"), I think it's high time that the government of Canada gave us Swedes recognition for the truly unique minority group that we are.

It's not easy being a Swede, I can tell you, and retaining our heritage is a full-time job. Thank goodness, there are still those large blue and yellow cultural centers, cleverly disguised as retail stores, where we Swedes can continue to teach our children Swedish as a second language. Here you will find descriptive words like "Snorr," and important phrases like "*tillverkat* I Hong Kong."

But, more than that, I think Canada as a whole should show us more respect for our ancient culture by becoming Swede-sensitized. For instance, it isn't politically correct to say, "Big Dumb Swede" anymore. We object to that. You now have to say, "Tall, mathematically challenged, gorgeous blonde Northern European with sky-blue eyes." (You should be so lucky!)

And it's not appropriate to call every Swede "Ole" either, especially if it's a girl, and her real name is Selma.

It seems to me that there are a whole lot of Swedish stereotypes which need to addressed, such as the assumption that all Swedes ski, herd reindeer, and run naked through snow banks beating their interesting parts with birch branches. These are simply not true. I, for one, don't even ski.

And—you tell me—why is it that it's always those Scots who get to pipe people into a room for ceremonial occasions? I know two or three accordion players who would die for the chance to schottische the governor general through a black tie crowd right up to the head table.

Take our national dress—do Swedes need permission to

127

wear their horned helmets and carry battle axes to work? I don't think so!

And don't forget the importance of our national holidays. We want *Midsommar* officially recognized so that our kids can stay up all night dancing, and learn to make pickled herring the old way.

Furthermore, come to think of it, it should be our inherent right to get our coffee duty free.

I think I've made my case, but if you need further proof that the Vikings preceded just about every other ethnic group in the New World, it is recorded in an old Norse legend that when the Swedish King Volvo I choked on a piece of lutefisk and gained admittance to Valhalla, he was buried with his favorite souvenirs: a package of bacon, two hockey sticks, and an Anne of Green Gables T-shirt.

Ya sure! You betcha! Swedes of Canada, unite!

Illustration by David Fitzsimmons

A Swedish Grandmother's Christmas Tradition

By Gail Carlson Mackay

In the play, *Tsimbali*, the mother tells her children that we observe our traditions so that we know who we are. My grandmother had a Christmas tradition which practically amounted to a family secret, because I don't think anyone but the family knew about it. I'm going to tell you about it anyway.

My grandmother's name was Anna Karolina, and she lived in Kenora, Ontario, Canada. Since all of her adult children moved, one by one, to Vancouver, she finally got the message, packed up her hardanger, and caught the Dominion West.

She loved to laugh, and could be quite wacky at times, saying everything with a lilting southern Swedish accent. We loved her dearly, and were delighted that she had come to stay.

Every year, her children, my aunts and uncles, took turns hosting the family Christmas Eve party, and the very year that Anna Karolina (Nana to us) moved to British Columbia, it happened to be our turn.

We ate Christmas dinner in the kitchen. Mother and Dad had to extend the seating arrangements by bringing up an old table from the basement, adding it to the existing arborite kitchen table, and covering the whole with two huge damask cloths. Wendy and I set the table with Mother's best Rogers plate, making two places at the end of the table for us. Since all the chairs in the house were for the adults, we shared the piano bench. Nana's place, of course, was set close to us.

"Gud Jul! Gud Jul! Merry Christmas," we heard from the porch. The family arrived just as we got the table ready, bringing gifts and food, and heavy coats to lay on Mother's bed.

When everyone was seated, Dad lit the candles which he had set into a small log, and Mother turned off the kitchen lights except for the one over the stove.

Between the Ukrainians and Swedes in our family, we always had homemade bread, cabbage rolls, perogies, ham, sil (pickled herring), Nana's headcheese, and a huge turkey — a turkey so huge that my dad and his brother had to extract it from the oven with the Jaws of Life. So we watched the meal progress with crackers to pull, pickles to slurp, and stories of Christmas before this one.

After the nuclear hot mince tarts, and snowballs made from icing sugar and mashed potatoes and chocolate shot (I think!), my aunts, Nana and the rest of us cleared the table and began the massive task of washing up and putting away. Nana started singing, "Nu Ar Det Jul Igen" ("Now It Is Christmas Again") in Swedish which made the work go faster.

Finally, we joined the men in the living room, bringing a plate of Nana's pepparkakor (gingerbread cookies), and a pot of strong coffee. Dad plugged in the Christmas tree and lit the fire in the Squamish rock fireplace.

Pretty soon, my uncles and aunts began teasing and telling stories about each other. The more we laughed, the more outrageous they became. Nana knitted and listened to the clowning around. Then my uncle Arol said, "So, Mother, are you going to stand on your head this Christmas, or are you getting too old?"

Nana put down her knitting, and said, "Minnie, you come with me for a minute." They disappeared into my parents' bedroom. Shortly after that, Nana reappeared, wearing a pair of my dad's trousers. She walked to the center of the room, and, kneeling, put her head and hands onto the yellow center of the braided rug. Then, very steadily, she lifted her feet into the air, and did a perfect head stand in the middle of the room.

Everyone clapped and laughed. My sister and I were stunned. This was our grandmother? My dad laughed so hard at the looks on our faces, his blue eyes had to blink away the tears. "It's a Carlson TRADITION," he explained, "my mother always stands on her head at Christmas!"

I'm not sure what that says about my family's idea of tradition, but the amazing Anna Karolina stood on her head for us every year after that, eventually doing it in the corner of the room where, her children insisted, it was safer.

I can still hear her saying, "By yimminy, I'm not so old that I can't stand on my head THIS Christmas!"

Swedish Gasoline

By Robin Ouren

If you didn't know better, you would swear on a stack of Lutheran hymnbooks that coffee was invented in Scandinavia. Those growing up in a Scandinavian community, where coffee is second only to God, have a hard time picturing some bronzed South American named Juan out picking the precious beans. It seems more plausible to believe that little coffee bushes thrive on northern hillsides, along with reindeer, trolls, and blondes on skis.

Swedes, especially, worship the grounds that coffee spills on. They are sitting in their "Carl Larssonesque" dining rooms, hands cupped around a mug of the strongest brew you've ever tasted. They call it Swedish gasoline.

Swedes know that their coffee is about right when a spoon stands up in the mix. If the spoon disintegrates, it's maybe a bit too potent even for them. Or maybe not?

Swedes in the United States are just as hot for the brown beverage. Stanton, Iowa is a village of about 700 souls, located in the very southwest corner of the state. Stanton was settled by Swedes in the mid-1800s, and the coffee tradition has been a part of life ever since. In 1971, the town even erected a monument to the brew the residents equate with Swedish hospitality. In that year, the town of Stanton refurbished their water storage tank. A nice handle, spout, lid, and some Swedish dala painting on the sides, and you have what looks like the biggest percolator you've ever laid eyes on. Stanton has come to be known as "The Town with the Swedish Coffee Pot."

According to Donald Peterson, president of the Stanton Historical Society, the idea for a coffee pot water tower was originally brewed there. However, there are some copy cats. Or is that copy pots? You can see a couple at a truck stop in Omaha, Nebraska, but they aren't as fancy. There's also one in the Scandinavian community of Kingsburg, California." They came later," says Peterson.

Stanton also has the distinction of being the hometown of the late actress Virginia Christine, better known as Mrs. Olson of coffee commercial fame. Oh, yes, you know her. She's the one who always said, "It's mountain grown." Christine was, of course, Swedish—on her mother's side.

Swedish gasoline! These days, many health-conscious Swedes are turning to the unleaded variety, but it's still coffee, and the pungent aroma wafts through the little town of Stanton accenting Swedish heritage.

Coffee pot
watertower
Stanton, Iowa

Betrayed by Geese

By Dana Lumby

On November 11, tribute is paid to the Bishop of Tours, Saint Mårten, soldier saint, who died in the year 387. The joyful tradition of celebrating Mårten *Gås* Day is still alive in America as well as Sweden, especially among the people of Skåne.

Mårten of Tours entered the Roman army when he was only fifteen. On a very cold winter day, he and his comrades came upon a beggar dressed in rags. The freezing man was passed by until Mårten saw him. Mårten drew his sword and cut his own cloak in half, giving the beggar the other half. A few years later, Mårten left the army and became a disciple of St. Hilary, the Bishop of Poitiers, France. Because of his strong opposition to the Arian heretics, Mårten had to go into exile. Later, when asked by the people of Tours to become bishop, he refused.

Legend says Mårten took refuge in a goose pen. The honking geese betrayed his hiding place, and members of his diocese, against his will, forced his installation as bishop. Despite his lack of desire to become bishop, he worked hard, and performed many pious and charitable acts.

On St. Mårten's Eve, November 10, the saint gets his revenge when flocks of geese, on the plains of Skåne in southern Sweden, are thinned out and the Mårten *Gås* readied for roasting on the 11th. Many tourists join in the feasting of roast goose, black soup (*svartsoppa* may or may not be served), and the classic side dishes. St. Mårten is considered also to be the patron saint of gastronomy, which may have come about because his saint day falls after the harvest when there is a bounty of food and wine, and the geese are plump.

In the Chicago area, the Swedish-American neighborhood of Andersonville, Illinois, starts the St. Mårten's *Gås* Day festivities on November 10, with the feasting and traditional symbols of prosperity and good cheer continuing through the December 13 Lucia celebrations and on through Christmas Day. During this time, the streets are decorated and filled with song, and the shops laden with special treats.

AROSIÆ Secundavice
Typis Consistorij, An. 1647.

"Woodblock print
of rooster"

Swedish Crafts:
Notes about Goats & Chickens

by Joan Liffring-Zug Bourret

The Swedes have straw goats and dala horses. This may be a rumor, but the Japanese wanted to manufacture the dala horse and the Swedish government said only Swedes can produce dala horses and only Swedes do. There are some American Swedes carving very similar horses.

There is a wonderful vignette of a major American importer of straw goats who discovered, on a shipment from Sweden, that someone had forgotten to remove a label "made in Taiwan" or "made in China." The importer then went to a trade show in the Far East and, of course, ran into the Swedes from Sweden. A fitting scene: straw goats in the Far East surrounded by Swedes and an American Swede stunned at finding each other there!

Charming chickens, carved from scraps of wood from the forests of Sweden, show the importance of the rooster as a symbol there. Dala carvings of big roosters come from the province of Dalarna. A cousin, who is mainly Irish, came to visit us and proudly displayed his whittling of a similar chicken. We screamed in protest—an Irish-American copying Swedish roosters! The power is inherent in the Swedish symbol.

Dala rooster

*Swedish carvings
from scraps of wood*

Defining Danes

By Robin Ouren

One of the most famous sons of Denmark is the melancholy Dane himself, Hamlet. The authentic life of this man inspired William Shakespeare to write the tragedy "Hamlet" in 1600. It revolves around Hamlet's seeking to avenge the death of his father, the king. The question is, was Hamlet a typical Dane? Let's see:

Denmark is a bridge between the Scandinavian countries and the continent of Europe. The resulting European influence seems to make Danes a little more outgoing than the rest of the Scandinavian pack. Hamlet certainly was outgoing. He was out in the garden at midnight going after a ghost. He was out going after everyone in sight to avenge his father's death. Yes, he was outgoing.

Danes are also more expressive than the more stoic breeds of Scandinavia. Hamlet was expressive. He expressed himself time and again with soliloquies and accusations and contemplations. His expressiveness takes up at least half of the play.

"Anything is good in moderation." This motto is a model for Danes in all that they do — exercising, working, eating, playing. Hamlet kills several people in this play, and then dies himself in great dramatic style. While this activity is expressive — "...ay, there's the rub..." (Hamlet) — it does not display moderation. By the final curtain, practically everybody in the play dies for one reason or another. This is obviously overkill and is not very Danish. The verdict: Mr. Shakespeare was English.

Aside from distinct personal qualities, Danes have other unique tastes. The food in Denmark, unlike usual Scandinavian fare, tends to be spicy — this, too, a result of European influence. Garlic is common, as is basil, oregano, parsley, sage, rosemary, and thyme. Several of these spices are mentioned by Ophelia in "Hamlet." In her mad scene, she says: "There's rosemary, that's for remembrance;..." and "There's fennel for you, and columbines; there's rue for you, and here's some for me; we may call it herb of grace o' Sundays;..."

A favorite Danish food is *Leverpostej* or liver pâté. That's chopped liver and a generous helping of fat—bacon, lard, or something equally delicious—spread onto dark rye bread. Pâté is easily 50-percent fat and very bad for the arteries. It is as common in Denmark as peanut butter is in the United States.

Christmas time brings uniquely Danish traditions. Danes trim their trees with paper hearts. Families and friends have cut-and-paste parties, designing and weaving together the intricate red-and-white hearts. Red and white, the colors of the Danish flag, add a sense of nationalism to the holiday. Danish Christmas trees also hold real candles, lit on Christmas Eve. Danes gather at the tree, join hands, and walk around the tree singing traditional hymns and carols. It is a magical atmosphere — watching the candles burn until the last candle is out and guessing which one that might be.

Tivoli Garden in Copenhagen, one of the most famous places in Denmark, is a kind of antique Disneyland offering boat rides, fine foods, entertainment, and a showcase of Danish culture. Real Danes pronounce it "ti-OH-li—very soft on the "V," accent on the "O." Native Danes trek to Tivoli every year or so, and tourists from around the world put it at the top of their travel agendas. Park benches, concerts, fireworks at midnight, and season passes maintain a typical Danish moderation.

Among best known Danish sons are nineteenth-century Danish writer Hans Christian Andersen, famous for fairy tales, and Søren Kierkegaard, nineteenth-century religious philosopher. Danes can tell you that Kierkegaard's works are existentialist, dark, and impassioned. Kierkegaard did not write with moderation. So maybe he isn't a typical Dane, but I think he would have gotten on well with Hamlet.

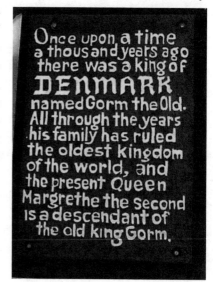

Once upon a time a thousand years ago there was a king of DENMARK named Gorm the Old. All through the years his family has ruled the oldest kingdom of the world, and the present Queen Margrethe the Second is a descendant of the old king Gorm.

Sign in Solvang, California

A *few words to the* "Wannabes"

By Robin Ouren

I hate to break the news to you, but not everyone is Scandinavian. It is true. But, those who are not certainly want to be, and do all sorts of things hoping that some Scandi-*nish* will rub off on them. This year, I ran into some friends one evening at Nordic Fest in Decorah, Iowa. They came to see the Nordic Dancers, a group of students from elementary through high school who work long and hard to perform authentic Scandinavian dances like schottisches and reels for the masses that attend the fest each July.

These friends — Maxine and Marlene — go back to junior high days. They happen to be twins. And, despite the fact that their last name is Johnson, they also happen to be Irish and Scottish, not that I hold that against them. Marlene is married to an Irish-German with a still-hanging-on New York accent, though he has lived in Iowa or Arizona for several years now. Not that I hold it against her, or him. He is named Ed. Ed is from New York City.

Max and Mar and Ed and baby Taji came to Nordic Fest, and being supper time, they were hungry. I can sympathize with all of you wannabes out there. No one expects you to understand Scandinavians. And we certainly can't cringe when you massacre pronunciations, especially of our delicious foods. With names like *ruiseipä* (Finnish rye bread) and *kræmmerhuse* (Danish cones, a dessert pastry with whipped cream filling and jelly on top) I suppose it is inevitable.

Ed and crew and I wandered over to Water Street where all of the fest food booths were set up. *Varme Pølser* sounded good to me, and after explaining this sausage wrapped in lefse treat to the others, we all ordered. Next came dessert. I asked Ed, "Have you ever eaten *rømmegrøt*?" Pronounced RUMugrut. Ed said, "Eaten what? Rubber granite?" I said, "No, rømmegrøt." He replied, "That's what I said, 'Rubber granite!' "

We proceeded onward to the "rubber granite" booth, where Irish-German Ed from New York, proceeded to order. "I'd like four bowls of 'rubber granite,' please." The woman in the booth looked at us funny. After my face returned to its normal color, I said, "He's not Norwegian." As if this was not already obvious.

Ed and crew liked "rubber granite," I mean, *rømmegrøt*, and they went on their merry way, sampling other delicacies. I went home, tired after a long, hot day of being an Art Fair vendor, the *pølser* and *rømmegrøt* pulsing through my veins and restoring my Scandinavian strength.

Sure, we put up with a lot of stuff from you "wannabes." We tolerate the jokes, excuse the mispronunciations, and humor your wearing plastic viking helmets with horns on them (viking helmets never had horns, or gull wings either for that matter) and the list goes on. But, that's okay, because we appreciate your enthusiasm and interest in us.

The legendary Jimmy Durante once said, "Everybody wants to get into the act!" If "the act" is being Scandinavian, who wouldn't?

Lena's Advice to "Wannabes"

Defy the "no horns" historians and get a helmet such as this one worn by Donna Bergen, manager of the Gift Shop at Vesterheim, Norwegian-American Museum, Decorah, Iowa.

Lena's Advice to"Wannabes"

✔ If the subject is grasshoppers, tell about St. Urho.
✔ Be a fan of Finland's sport of "Wife Carrying." Contestants carry mates over an obstacle course of sand, asphalt, grass, through a waist high pool and over two fences. To discourage lightweights, the prize is the woman's weight in beer.
✔ If asked about horns, aggressively respond that horned helmets were worn in the Bronze Age, 1000 to 500 B.C.

✔ Debate, with passion, the authenticity, of the Runestone.
✔ Tell Ole jokes.
✔ Keep canned lutefisk handy for emergencies.*
✔ Eat Nordic Foods at festivals.

Illustration by David Fitzsimmons

*Publisher Joan Liffring-Zug Bourret spooned steaming yellow chunks of "pineapple" onto her plate in a buffet line. Alas! buttered lutefisk, masquerading!

Lori Breszee and Lucille Setz at Syttende Mai, *Stoughton, Wisconsin*

Lena's Advice to "Wannabes"
Discover Folk Art

Elaborate jigsaw work, painted birds and birdhouses, angels and doves highlight this clock case carved by Christian Alfred Hendrickson (1879-1961). Gift to Vesterheim* from the Aase Haugen Home in Decorah.

Birdhouse made in 1930s by Ole Kragness, Oppedal, Norway, maternal grandfather of donor to Vesterheim, Merrill G. Swenson, Harvey, Louisiana. Built on the lid of a wooden herring keg and finished with asphalt shingles, it incorporates architectural features from traditional Norwegian stave churches and stabburs or storehouses.

*Vesterheim means "western home" in Norwegian.

Discover Vesterheim

"Ed"
Stearns County Farmer
Milks Cow, Drinks Beer

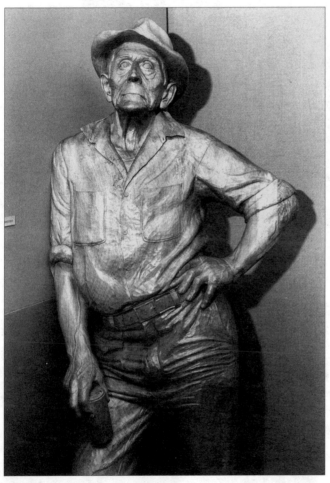

Sculpture of a Norwegian-American farmer, made in 1986 from silver maple, by sculptor Fred Cogelow, Willmar, Minnesota. Model reportedly found in the frozen-food section of a supermarket. Purchased by Vesterheim Trustees in 1991 and given as a gift in honor of Lila and Marion John Nelson on their retirement as Curator of Textiles and Director of Vesterheim.

Lena's Advice to "Wannabes"
Attend Festivals—they're nationwide.
Wear your statement with pride!

Høstfest, *Minot, South Dakota*

Cultivate a love for lutefisk!
Enter a lutefisk eating contest at the Nordic Fest, Decorah, Iowa.

BOOKS BY MAIL: (Price does not include shipping.)
1997 prices subject to change.

Joyful Nordic Humor: A Family Album (this book) $16.95
The Best of Queen Lena by Charlene Powers (our cover girl) $12.95

Recipes, History, Culture and Tradition
 Definitely Danish: History, Culture, Recipes $10.95
 Delectably Danish: Recipes and Reflections $7.95
 Fantastically Finnish: Recipes and Traditions $7.95
 Notably Norwegian: Recipes, Festivals, Folk Arts $7.95
 Superbly Swedish: Recipes and Traditions $7.95
 Time Honored Norwegian Recipes $12.95

Proverb Series: $10.95 each; three for $25
 Danish Proverbs
 Finnish Proverbs
 Norwegian Proverbs
 Proverbs from the North: Words of Wisdom from the Vikings
 Swedish Proverbs

Folklore and Adventure
 Fish of Gold and Other Finnish Folk Tales $7.95
 Scandinavian Ghost Stories $12.95
 Trolls Remembering Norway $12.95
 Voyage of the Tradewind: Norway to America $8.95
 Weird Tales from Northern Seas by Jonas Lie $10.95
 Traditional designs by Helen Blanck: *Flowers of Dalarna,* $12.95;
 Rosemaling, Beautiful Norwegian Art, $12.95; *Rosemaling Design
  Collection #2* $12.95

Literature
 Best of Finnish Americana $14.95
 Carl Larsson: Autobiography of Sweden's Most Beloved Artist $16.95
 FinnFun by Bernhard Hillila $12.95
 Forbidden Fruit and Other Stories by Juhani Aho $12.95
 My Story: Inkeri's Journey by Inkeri Väänänen-Jensen $12.95

Selma Lagerlöf Series
 Girl from the Marsh Croft $12.95
 Gösta Berling's Saga $16.95
 Invisible Links $12.95
 Memories of Mårbacka $16.95
 *Three Stories: Scandinavian Kings and Queens
  Astrid, Sigrid Störrade, The Silver Mine* $10.95
 Words of Wisdom from Selma Lagerlöf $10.95

"Stocking Stuffers"
 Mini-Recipe Books (5 1/2"x 3 1/2"), 120 to 160 pages $5.95 each
 Dear Danish Recipes   *Scandinavian Sweet Treats*
 Fine Finnish Foods   *Scandinavian Smorgasbord*
 Norwegian Recipes   *Splendid Swedish Recipes*
 Scandinavian Holiday Recipes

Complete Catalog: $2.50
   Penfield Press — 215 Brown Street — Iowa City, Iowa 52245

Toll free number 1-800-728-9998

Dala Painting
Swedish Floral Painting

from The Flowers of Dalarna
by Helen Elizabeth Blanck

"Just for fun!"
Norwegian Rosemaling Design

from Rosemaling Design Collection #2
by Helen Elizabeth Blanck